Look on the Bright Side

Daily Rays of Hope for Tough Times

April Crimbley

April Crimbley Books

Copyright © 2025 by April Crimbley

All rights reserved.

No portion of this book may be used or reproduced by any means, graphic, electronic, or mechanical, including photocopying, recording, taping or by any information storage retrieval system without the written permission of the publisher except in the case of brief quotations embodied in critical articles and reviews.

Published by April Crimbley Books

ISBN: 978-1-7334011-3-5 (pbk)
ISBN: 978-1-7334011-4-2 (ebk)

Printed in the United States of America.

Scripture quotations, unless otherwise indicated, are taken from the HOLY BIBLE, NEW LIVING TRANSLATION and NEW INTERNATIONAL VERSION®. NIV ® Copyright © 1973, 1978, 1984 by International Bible Society. Used by permission of Zondervan Publishing House. All rights reserved.

The "NIV" and "New International Version" trademarks are registered in the United States Patent and Trademark Office by International Bible Society. Use of either trademark requires the permission of the International Bible Society.

Cover by Delia Gains and Prudence Makhura

Editing by Michelle Chester, www.ebm-services.com

For everyone who ever feels down, I hope and pray that you will read something on these pages that will help you see the bright side of any situation you face.

To my husband, Nate—Your love and support mean everything.
To my daughter, Chari'—Your joy lights up my world. Keep spreading your light.
To my sister, Lenora—Your optimism is a gift. You always see the bright side of every situation.
To my friend, Shirley—This book would not exist without your spark of an idea.

How to Use This Book

Find hope and strength right at your fingertips!

Keep *Look on the Bright Side* nearby—on your desk, nightstand, or coffee table. Be ready to flip through its pages anytime you need a boost.

You will get inspirational stories, practical advice, relevant Bible verses, and starter prayers for those difficult times in your life.

Each section includes daily affirmations and questions for personal reflection to help reinforce the message presented.

You can read *Look on the Bright Side* daily, or you can skip to the section you need based on the specific topic.

Keep this book handy for reference, and consider keeping a journal nearby for your thoughts.

Enjoy!

Contents

1. Introduction — 1
2. When You Need a Jumpstart — 5
3. When You Are Feeling Down — 15
4. When Your Self-esteem is Low — 25
5. When You Are Worried — 45
6. When You Are Anxious — 59
7. When You Are Afraid — 69
8. When You Are Confused — 77
9. When It's Hard to Forgive — 87
10. When It's Hard to Forgive Yourself — 99
11. When You Are Mourning — 107
12. When Life Seems Hopeless — 117
13. When You Are Lonely — 129
14. When You Are Struggling with Being Single — 139
15. When You Are Struggling with Marriage — 149
16. When You Have Been Hurt — 161

17.	When You Are Sick	169
18.	When You are Discontent	179
19.	When You Are Having Trouble at Work	189
20.	When You Are Dealing with Difficult People	199
21.	When You Are Concerned About Aging	207
22.	Conclusion	221
	About the Author	224
	Also by April Crimbley	225

CHAPTER 1

Introduction

As I prepared to leave work that day, my cell phone rang with a call from the nurse. "You need to come in and get a biopsy. We see lumps in your breast on the mammogram. We need to see if the lumps are cancerous." She quickly answered my questions, scheduled the appointment, and then hung up.

I was in shock.

As I walked to my car, my mind was bombarded with negative thoughts:

Oh no, what if I have breast cancer?

Am I going to die?

Is it my time to go?

I was terrified.

Over the next few weeks, even though I prayed about it, my mind was consumed with worry. I was distraught over the fact that I could be dying and would be leaving my family. I felt like a dark cloud was following me everywhere I went.

By the time my doctor's appointment came for the biopsy, I was nervous. I didn't know what to expect, but, when I lay on the hospital bed to prepare for the procedure, I suddenly felt an overwhelming sense of peace.

I felt as if God's presence was right there in the room with me, assuring me that everything would be alright.

The doctor performed the biopsy in minutes. The whole procedure was easier than I had expected. Thank God I received good news—there was no cancer. The lumps were only benign cysts.

I am so grateful for the good news. Through this experience, I gained a whole new perspective on and appreciation for life.

That experience, along with many others, taught me how to look on the bright side of every situation. Despite all my worrying and negative thoughts, everything turned out well. Worrying doesn't accomplish anything so you might as well focus on the positive.

Looking on the bright side doesn't mean walking around wearing rose-colored glasses in your own fairytale world. It doesn't mean ignoring the problems. Rather, looking on the bright side means acknowledging the problem, doing your part to improve it, and focusing on the positive—knowing that God is always with you.

Every situation has a bright side. As you read *Look on the Bright Side*, be prepared to reflect on your own situations and find ways to stay positive and look on the bright side of whatever challenges you face.

CHAPTER 2

When You Need a Jumpstart

Great things are waiting for you!

Christmas Day was always an exciting time for my sisters, my brothers, and me when we were children. Even though my mom's income was limited, we were rich in love and happiness, and she always showered us with lots of gifts at Christmas.

On the night before Christmas, we would each open one gift. Then, early on Christmas morning, we would wake up and run to the living room to open the rest of the presents under the tree.

I remember one Christmas morning when I opened a gift to find a toy sewing machine. I was so happy to see a tiny pink version of the sewing machine my mom used to make clothes and do alterations. Just like kids on Christmas Day, we should wake up every single morning expecting something wonderful to happen. We should approach each day looking for something new and thrilling.

Every new day brings an opportunity for something great to happen—you never know what could happen. A big surprise or something you never imagined could possibly take place in your life. You might receive an unexpected check in the mail. You could earn a job offer for your dream job. You could get an opportunity to buy a new home. You never know—you could meet someone who becomes a lifelong friend or partner.

Keep your eyes open for great prospects. Let go of any inhibitions and partialities that might prevent you from recognizing a blessing. Sometimes, the gift you receive looks different from what you expected. You may not even realize you needed it until it arrives.

When you get up in the morning, be open to new and unique possibilities. God loves you deeply and wants the best for you. When unexpected blessings come into your life, receive them freely without hesitation.

Expect great things in your life!

Every day is a special gift.

You've been tossing and turning in bed all night, and you finally drift off to sleep. You're in a deep slumber when the alarm suddenly wakes you up.

Slowly, you open your eyes and think, *"Is it morning already?"* You press the snooze button a few times before rolling your lifeless body out of bed.

Sometimes, getting up in the morning is hard. The world can feel dark with so much tragedy, loss, and uncertainty.

When you wake up in the morning, ask yourself, How can I make this a great day? Every day you wake up is a gift. Try starting the day with a grateful heart. Jumpstarting your day with gratefulness will prepare you for whatever challenges may come your way.

Seeing each morning as a special gift sets the tone for your day, allowing you to approach things in a positive light. The gift of life is such a precious thing. At any given moment, we could leave this earth—none of us will live forever.

Time flies by so quickly. Before you know it, years will have flown by. Until you say goodbye to this world, you should do your best to enjoy every waking moment.

Maybe your day involves working, going to school, traveling, helping someone in need, or visiting a homebound loved one. Whatever you do, treasure the day. Do everything with love and a pleasant attitude. Since you've committed to doing your responsibilities, you might as well make the best of every waking moment.

I have found that starting my day with prayer and inspirational music sets the tone. When I dedicate my day to God, I have the energy to make it through whatever comes my way. It's like I'm putting my day in His hands. Listening to my favorite music lifts my spirits and gives me the motivation I need.

God gives you the gift of a brand-new day to do whatever you want with it. Choose how you will embrace it.

Every day is a day to be cherished.

Babies are precious, and we cherish them because they are so tiny, innocent, and helpless. Family heirlooms are cherished because they hold treasured history and are passed down through generations. To cherish something means you protect and care for it lovingly.

When you protect something, you defend it and don't allow anything to harm it. Protecting something means safeguarding it from any potential harm.

There are only so many hours in a day. Here are some ways to celebrate each one:

- **Fill each hour with gratitude.** Spend your hours engaging in activities that allow you to enjoy life as much as possible

- **Protect your day from anything that might diminish your happiness.** If you are in a position at work that you do not enjoy, try to find something positive within that environment. Don't let the environment bring you down

- **Safeguard your mental well-being if you are in a challenging phase in a relationship**. Seek ways to protect your peace until you and your partner find a way to improve things.

- **Find ways to bring joy into your heart if you are surrounded by negativity.** Protect your peace of mind by praying for strength and joy. When possible, step away from the negativity and visit your happy place.

Cherish each day by lovingly expressing gratitude to God for allowing you to see another day. Care lovingly for your day by praying for guidance on how to glorify God in your life in this new day.

A new day brings new opportunities.

I love watching the sunrise. As the sun slowly appears above the horizon, the sky displays a range of colors—yellow, orange, red, pink, and blue. The sunrise symbolizes peace, serenity, and the start of a new day.

Anything could happen in each new day you are given. Only God knows what could happen in your life as you start your day. Something amazingly wonderful could happen that would knock you off your feet.

God sees the big picture of your life and knows every little thing about you. He knows every door you will walk through. He knows your beginning and your end. God wants to bless you and fill your life with joy and peace. Everything you need is in His hands.

With each new day, you have time to do something meaningful. The fact that you are alive and breathing gives you the opportunity to write the book you always wanted to write, travel to the foreign place you wanted to visit, or start school to get a college degree.

The day has been given to you to live. No one can live it for you. You can do whatever you want on this day that you have been blessed with. If it is a work day, you may have opportunities to interact with others—interactions that could turn into divine opportunities, leading to experiences that enrich your life.

There have been times when I gained valuable insight that led to financial growth from a short chat with a stranger. I have learned helpful tips that increased my wellness because of conversations with people I met only briefly at work.

Keep your eyes and ears open to new opportunities that await you. There is always a possibility of gaining helpful information from people you don't know.

As long as you are alive, opportunities are endless for you. It's up to you to choose what you want to do with your day.

A new day is another opportunity for you to shine your light.

It doesn't matter how dark a room is, a light will always show the way. You can choose to walk in the dark, or you can flip the switch to turn on the light. Every day that you wake up, you have a choice: you could be a light to everyone around you, or you can hide your light.

There is a lot of darkness in the world—wars, violence, and tragedies—but there is also a lot of light when we show love and kindness.

Light adds. Darkness subtracts.

Choose to add light and positivity into your environment, wherever you are. It doesn't matter how dark your work or personal situation is, you can always add light. It only takes a small amount of light to brighten the darkness.

Words are powerful. They can add light in dark situations. Responding with kindness to someone's negativity can diffuse conflict and bring positivity to the situation. It is not necessary to respond to unkind words with more unkind words. Sometimes, responding with pleasant words can make a significant difference in the outcome of the situation.

You could bring light to a dark situation by speaking positive words. The next time someone tries to provoke you with harsh words, respond with kindness. Shower them with love and sweetness until they have no choice but to reciprocate.

If they continue to speak hateful words, respond with love and kindness. If you cannot find any kind words to say, remain silent and allow them to vent. Sometimes, people just need to release pain that comes from somewhere else. Even though you are not to blame, you can help them heal by allowing them to express their anger or frustration.

Share as much love and kindness as you can. Your world and everyone else around you will be a better place when you shine your light.

Personal Reflection

How will I jumpstart my day when I feel sluggish?

Prayer to Jumpstart Your Day

Heavenly Father, thank You for waking me up this morning.
I am so grateful that You blessed me with another day.
Thank You for watching over me as I slept last night. I praise You for another day
and another opportunity to live for You.
Please go before me in everything I say and do in this day.
I pray that You will lead me and guide me into the paths that You have for me.
I pray for divine appointments.
I pray for Your angels of protection to surround me.
I pray that Your love will shine through me to everyone I meet.
Thank You, Lord. Amen.

Bible Verse to Jumpstart Your Day

The faithful love of the Lord never ends! His mercies never cease.
Great is his faithfulness; his mercies begin afresh each morning.
Lamentations 3:22-23

CHAPTER 3

When You Are Feeling Down

Storms are only temporary.

I was traveling to Tennessee from Georgia when a heavy rainstorm begins. The rain was so intense that the visibility was getting worse and worse. I was driving on a stretch of interstate that wound along a mountain full of twists, turns, and blind spots.

The interstate I was on is one of the most treacherous highways in the United States.

As the storm intensified and the rain fell harder, I considered pulling over until it slowed down, but there was no roadside space to do so. I was surrounded by 18-wheeler trucks, which made visibility even worse as rain splashed on my windshield when they passed.

It was one of the scariest moments of my life. All I could do was drive slowly and pray. I kept repeating to myself, "You can make it through this."

When I finally drove through the storm, there was sunshine on the other side. It was so beautiful. Just moments before, I had been driving through dark clouds, loud thunder, heavy rain, and strong winds along a winding mountain highway. Then, I saw the sun. I was overcome with relief and joy.

Life is like that. Sometimes, we experience dark storms with heavy rain. Those moments can be terrifying. We face situations where we don't know how we'll make it through. But we keep pushing forward, and eventually, we reach the other side and see the sun.

Maybe you're experiencing a dark time right now. Don't worry, you will make it through. It might be raining hard in your life right now and you can barely see your way. The clouds are dark and may seem endless, but if you push through the storm, you will see the sunshine.

Don't give up. Keep moving. Keep praying. Keep believing.

You will emerge victorious on the other side.

Jesus is only a prayer away.

When traveling, some trips take a few hours, while others take much longer. Sometimes, layovers and airport delays disrupt getting to your destination.

Cell phone usage is not allowed on planes because signals could interfere with the aircraft's communication system and the air traffic control. If you need to make a phone call, you have to wait until the plane lands.

The wonderful news about Jesus is that you don't have to travel to reach Him. He is always with you. Even if you travel clear across the world, you can call on Jesus anytime—day or night—and it won't cost you a thing.

When you feel down or lonely, just whisper a prayer to Jesus, and He will hear you. You don't have to drive to a hands-free cell phone location. You don't have to wait for hours for the plane to land. He is always there.

You have permission to pray with no restrictions and no limits. All you have to do is talk to God as if He were your friend. You don't have to wait for a strong internet connection—His signal is clear, available, and waiting for you.

You won't be placed on hold and forced to wait. God is always listening to every word you say.

God never sleeps. He never takes a nap. He is wide awake, waiting to hear from you. It doesn't matter what language you speak. He understands. Even when you don't know what to say, God knows what's in your heart.

Don't worry about using fancy words. God has no favoritism for big words, loud empty prayers, or religious rhetoric. If you don't know what to say, you could use the prayer "template" that Jesus gave that starts with "Our Father, which art in heaven."

The next time you feel down or in despair, know that Jesus cares. All it takes is one prayer, one whisper, one call for help. He is already there, just waiting for you to call on Him.

Go to your happy place.

Do you have a happy place? Your happy place is wherever you go when you need a moment of happiness. It's the place that brings you peace.

Your happy place could be a room in your home reserved just for you, it could be jogging, going to the gym, listening to music, gardening, watching a movie at the theater, hiking, or simply sitting on your back porch.

Sometimes life gets so overwhelming that we need to break away and retreat to our happy place. What is yours?

Ask yourself these questions to find your happy place:

- What are some things you enjoy doing that make you happy?

- What is it that you enjoy doing that refreshes your emotional health?

- What can you do to nurture your true personality on a regular basis?

Going to your happy place is essential when you are going through a tough time because it brings peace and calm. It could also help improve your relationships—when you feel better, your relationship with others improves.

Visiting your happy place can boost your self-confidence; it reconnects you with your true self and reminds you of who you were created to be. When you feel reenergized and motivated, there is no limit to what you can accomplish.

God created you for a purpose. There is a space in this world that only you can fill. To fulfil that purpose, you must embrace your unique self. When you find yourself losing your true self, go to your happy place. Talk to your Creator and ask Him to refresh and restore your joy.

Reenergize the person you were created to be. Then, take active steps to do the things that bring you joy.

When you go to your happy place, you will be able to thrive with confidence.

Sing a song.

My first year in college was a sad time for me because I had moved away from my family to live on campus. Music helped me get through many lonely nights in my dorm room. When I played my favorite songs, they lifted my spirit.

Music has power. It can lift you up when you're feeling down. When you're sick and can barely get out of bed, music can feed your mind and spirit with the strength you need to recover.

Music can help soothe heartache and pain and help you to move forward. It can improve your mood and energy. Music can stir up all kinds of emotions, depending on what is stored in your memory bank.

If music can impact you in so many ways, imagine how much more powerful singing from your heart can lift you up. The next time you feel down, try singing a song and see how much better you will feel.

There are several stories in the Bible that show the power of music—David played his harp to sooth King Saul who was troubled; Joshua brought down the walls of Jericho with trumpets; Jehoshaphat and his army sang songs to defeat the enemy; Gideon and three hundred men blew trumpets in their battle. Even today we continue to witness the healing power of music.

Singing sends a positive spirit into the atmosphere and helps you to look on the bright side. Even more, singing a song to God from your heart creates a spirit of true worship. You will feel burdens lift when you sing songs to God. You may even sense the presence of the Holy Spirit, which is awesome because the Holy Spirit speaks to God on your behalf.

Joy will enter the room when you sing songs to your Heavenly Father. It doesn't matter how you sound.

The next time you are feeling down, or you are lying sick in bed, sing a song from your heart or play your favorite music, and you will feel better.

Someone is there to help you carry your load.

When heavy weightlifters work out, they usually have someone to assist them. This person is called a spotter. A spotter stands behind the weightlifter, helping to steady the dumbbells as they lift. The spotter ensures that the weightlifter can lift safely.

Sometimes, life can get so hard that it feels unbearable—like carrying a heavy weight.

Sometimes, you need a spotter in your life to help carry heavy burdens. There are people in your life who would be honored to help you carry your heavy load.

Who have you trusted with your private matters in the past? Who would be a good listener for you, to listen with compassion and grace? **Who do you have in your life to hold your struggles close to their heart in strict confidentiality?**

If you know someone strong enough to help you carry the load, reach out to them, and let them know you need their help. Don't try to carry the heavy weight alone.

Don't be ashamed to ask for a spotter. Pray and think about who you could trust to be a good listener. Then, ask for help so you can regain the strength to move forward.

If there is absolutely no one you feel you can trust, know that you are not alone. God is with you and will always help you carry any burden. He watches over you daily, waiting for you to hand the load over to Him.

God is not just a spotter—He will carry all the weight for you. You will be able to glide like an eagle because you will be so light after God takes the load from you.

Trust God and ask Him to help you with the heavy weights.

Personal Reflection

What can I do to lift myself up when I am feeling down?

Prayer for When You Are Feeling Down

Heavenly Father, I feel so down right now. My heart is heavy.
I don't have the words to explain how I feel. I feel alone.
The heaviness is almost unbearable.
I can't stand the pain that I'm feeling right now.
Please help me. Please lift this heavy burden.
Father, I am giving my cares and pain to You.
Please help me to make it through this.
Thank You for lifting my heavy hurt.
Thank You for pushing out the darkness and filling my heart with joy.
I praise You in advance for peace and happiness.
Thank You for easing my troubled mind.
Thank You for holding my hand and giving me the strength I need to carry on.
Amen.

Bible Verse for When You Are Feeling Down

> Praise the Lord, praise God our savior!
> For each day he carries us in his arms.
> Psalms 68:19

CHAPTER 4

When Your Self-esteem is Low

Explore your life purpose.

There is nothing that will give you more hope in tough times than knowing your life purpose.

When you hear the words "life purpose," you probably imagine a beam of light shining from heaven with a voice that says, "This is your life purpose."

I'll let you in on a secret: more than likely, you are already fulfilling your life purpose and don't even realize it. In other words, what you have to complete your life purpose is already inside you.

Your life purpose is directly connected to the gifts and talents that God has blessed you with.

Here are some questions to help you explore your life purpose:
What do you enjoy doing or enjoy learning to do?

Do you love working with your hands, writing, drawing, baking, or fixing things? Do you enjoy talking and engaging others in meaningful conversation? Do you love motivating people or singing?

The reason you have the desire to do or learn those things is because those desires were placed inside you, along with the gifts and talents to do them. God placed those gifts inside you so that you can help others. Ultimately, your gifts and talents are meant to help other people and to glorify your Creator. They are not yours to keep to yourself.

What strengths come easy to you that others might find difficult?

If you have trouble identifying your strengths, it's probably because they come so naturally for you. Your strengths are easy for you because they are your God-given talents.

Consider the following questions to discover your strengths:

When do you shine?

Do you shine when you cook dinner for your family? When you fix things? When you plan events, bake, sing, or write? What is something you truly excel at?

What do others tell you you're good at?

When people compliment you repeatedly on something, that is a good sign that you are pretty good.

What have you been asked to do?

Have you ever been asked to take on a particular task you didn't think you could—or wanted to—do, but once you started, you discovered how good you were at it? That's because the person who asked you saw your gifts and talents before you did.

Who are you passionate about helping? What group of people tug at your heart?

This is likely the group of people you were created to help. Your gifts and talents are tied to this group of people because you have been equipped to provide what they need in some capacity. For example, maybe you have a heart to help unhoused people, disadvantaged women, or children with special needs. Perhaps you're drawn to a group of people because they remind you of a personal hardship from your past. Your empathy could make meaningful differences in their lives when you use your gifts and talents to serve them.

Whoever you have compassion for is a strong clue as to what your life purpose is. Your heart tugs when you see or hear about them because their need is awakening the gifts inside you to help them.

Having a life purpose doesn't mean you have to save the entire world. Just use what's inside you and what's within your power—no matter how big or small you think it is.

Don't worry or fret about finding your life purpose. Just do your best to purposefully enjoy life.

Confirm your life purpose.

The key to confirming your life purpose is to take action. When you take that leap of faith, you will discover that your purpose was hidden there all along.

What has been on your heart to do? What have you been asked to do at work, in the community, or through a local church or organization? Say "yes" and you just might discover your purpose.

You may have experienced painful circumstances in your life. Even those situations can be used as part of your life purpose. There are numerous stories in the Bible that support this point. One of the most powerful is the story about Joseph, who ended up in a leadership position years after being left in a ditch by his brothers.

Here are some steps you can take to confirm your life purpose after exploring the areas discussed in the previous section.

Reflect on the last time you did something that made you feel excited, energized, and came easily to you.

This is a clue to your life purpose. When you are walking in your purpose, you don't have to force yourself, it flows naturally and often comes with a sense of divine guidance.

Maybe you weren't excited, but you were in a zone or in your element. Your gifts were placed inside you when God created you. When you are using the gifts He gave you, they will flow like a river. **Take the leap and try something.**

If there is a desire in your heart to start a baking business, volunteer with children, find a new job, write a book, launch a clothing line—go ahead and try it. That desire may be leading you to your life purpose.

Don't underestimate the power of your gift or life purpose.

Your purpose was designed to help build the kingdom of God—or, practically put, to make this world a better place. There are no small gifts when it comes to giving to others.

Never underestimate the value of any encounter you have with anyone. Every person you meet gives you an opportunity to touch someone's life in ways you may never imagine.

You may not see the big picture of what's going on in your life or in the world, but God does. He placed the gifts inside you to complete a piece of the greater puzzle in the huge world.

Live your life purpose.

Newsflash! Your life purpose is ultimately to glorify God.

You were placed on this earth and given gifts and talents because He trusted you to use them to help others—which, ultimately, glorifies Him.

Here are some clues that you are truly living your life purpose:

- You will use your gifts and talents with passion and enjoyment. Others will recognize your passion and will be drawn to you, especially the group of people you were created to help.

- You will feel a deep sense of validation in your heart. This is because you are fulfilling what you were created to do.

- You will get a "second wind" when you feel tired or discouraged. Activating your gifts and talents will give you energy when you need it most.

- Your empathy for the people you were created to help will energize you as you serve them. Your compassion for them will give you the drive you need to help them.

- You will be in a zone because you are in your element. When you are using the gifts you were blessed with, your energy will flow endlessly, like a river.

Once you realize your life purpose, your goal should be to purposely live accordingly. That means aligning all your life decisions with your purpose.

Take some time to get to know yourself and to confirm your gifts and talents. Do not minimize any strengths you possess. Every strength, gift, and talent you have can be used to help someone and ultimately glorify your Heavenly Father.

When you live your authentic self, your light will shine wherever you go.

Have you ever met someone who lights up the room the moment they walk in? That person seems to bubble over with sunshine.

A person who lights up the room has a vibrant and charismatic personality that makes other people feel happy.

You can be the person who transforms your environment when you allow your true personality to shine. When you do the things you enjoy doing, you will have strength and confidence in your step. You will shine when you are being your authentic self.

You might say, "Well, I'm not charismatic." But everyone has a unique personality and style. You may not have a charismatic personality, but when you do the things you enjoy doing, you will glow, and your glow will be contagious.

When you do the things you're good at—like singing, baking, fixing things—you'll do them with passion, and your passion will energize those around you. When you use the gifts and talents that God gave you, you will shine your light because His love will show through your personality.

If you've ever used your talents and gifts, you have likely experienced a wonderful feeling. That's because you were living out what you were created to do. In that moment, you were shining like a bright light. And that light creates an atmosphere of joy within you and with those around you.

You were not created to hide your light from the world. Your light is the gifts and talents you were blessed with to share with those around you. When you suppress your gifts, you hide the light that could make the world a better place.

Even if you don't reach the entire world, you are reaching someone within your surroundings.

Be yourself. Use the gifts and talents you were given. Shine your light.

There is a space in this world that only you can fill.

You are important because you were created for a reason that only you can fulfill.

You are the only one with your unique gifts, your unique personality, and your unique style. God wants to bless other people through your individuality. There is someone in this world who needs what only you can give through your talents.

Using the gifts and talents that God blessed you with to help others in some capacity will increase your self-esteem and also empower you to live with passion.

Be intentional about using your gifts and talents. Say "yes" when someone asks you to volunteer or take on a task that sounds unpredictable. It might lead to you discovering gifts and talents you didn't know you had.

When you spend time doing things that align with your personality, gifts, and talents, your self-esteem will rise because you will know you are doing what you were created to do.

Stay focused on your life purpose, and resist anything or anyone that tries to pull you away from your unique self. Life can throw a lot of things at you, but don't let distractions keep you from doing what you were born to do.

Do not compromise your purpose by doing things you should not do. Your vigor could become dull in how you approach things when you compromise who you are. When you are in the middle of a situation where you are tempted to compromise your values, remind yourself of your life purpose.

Don't try to be someone else. You might look good and sound good, but you won't be showcasing your true voice. If you try to imitate others, you won't connect with the people you were designed to reach because you will lack the passion needed to engage them.

Own the space you were created to fill. That space is yours to flourish in and to shine, so the world can see the wonderful things God can do through you. Show others how God can bless them too by using the gifts and talents He gave you.

Put God first in your life, follow your heart's desire, and you will walk in your purpose.

God's approval is the only approval you need.

There was a time in my life when I was part of an "organization" that required a certain way of dressing. The hardest part of abiding by those rules was the disapproving looks and condemning comments I would receive when someone saw me wearing forbidden attire.

After I left the organization, it took years for me to get rid of the feelings of guilt even though I was no longer there. I eventually gave myself freedom to wear what I want without feeling condemned.

Maybe you're in a position where someone else's approval impacts your lifestyle. It's okay to seek wise counsel from trusted people from time to time, but true internal peace comes from relying on God's approval for your final decisions.

Ultimately, God's approval is the only approval you need because He created you. When you seek God's approval:

- You will live a more authentic life because you won't be influenced by people's random and meaningless opinions.

- You won't succumb to society's pressures or criticism because you'll be confident in your decisions.

- Your priorities will shift from comparing yourself to others to pursuing your personal goals.

You receive God's approval the moment you allow Him to lead and guide you. His love and approval are unconditional.

Who are you ultimately living for?

It's okay to love yourself.

It's okay to love yourself and take care of yourself.

Jesus said, "*You must love the Lord your God with all your heart, all your soul, and all your mind. This is the first and greatest commandment. A second is equally important: Love your neighbor as yourself.*"

You can have a healthy measure of love for yourself when you put God first and love your neighbor. Self-care and self-love are not the same as idolizing yourself, putting yourself on a pedestal, and thinking you are more than you are. Loving yourself does not mean you think you are better than others.

Loving yourself means you appreciate the personality that God gave you and you intentionally use your gifts and talents to your full potential.

God gave you the gifts and talents you have to help others in one way or another. He wakes you up every morning and gives you life and breath. The best way to show gratitude for life is to glorify Him by using your gifts and talents.

Putting God first and loving the person He created you to be will give you the courage you need to make it in life. Faith in God and self-confidence will give you the motivation you need to pursue the career you want, start a business, have meaningful relationships, and reach other goals.

Part of loving and accepting yourself is the ability to identify your strengths. Your strengths are directly tied to the gifts and talents God blessed you with. There is nothing wrong with having confidence in the gifts and talents you were given.

Love yourself with no hesitation and be true to yourself—the person God created you to be.

Love and embrace your WHOLE self.

God created us in His image. Not only that, but He also made each one of us unique—in our own way. The Bible says that even the very hairs of our head are numbered. That means your Creator cares about every little detail of who you are. When God created you, He was intentional. Everything God created is good, and He created you.

You may not like the size of your nose or lips or the proportions of your body, but you are exactly who you are supposed to be. Maybe you wish you were smaller or larger than you are. Maybe your hair doesn't grow as long or isn't as straight or curly as you would like it to be.

Whatever your appearance, size, or personality, it is how God created you. Whether your size is due to health factors or not, you are who you are at this moment in your life. You are alive and breathing and therefore able to use the life and body that you've been given to move through life.

Embrace every part of who you are—inwardly and outwardly. Allow the most beautiful and authentic parts of your personality to shine when you present yourself to the world. Don't suppress any part of yourself out of fear of embarrassment or by comparing yourself with others. You are amazing and wonderful just the way you are because you were created by your amazing and wonderful Heavenly Father.

Yes, you are still growing and evolving. The longer you live, the better you will become, especially as you yield your life to God and ask for His strength in your areas of weakness. **Be patient with yourself as you work on yourself.**

With God's help, you will eventually get to where you want to be. In the meantime, love and embrace yourself for who you are—both the good parts and also what you consider to be the bad parts.

You are needed in the puzzle of life.

You are a very important person because you are here and breathing. The fact that you exist means that God created you for a reason. Everything and everyone God created was made with purpose.

Think of life as a puzzle. Every piece, or every person, is needed to create a beautiful picture. If even one piece is missing, the picture will be incomplete. You are needed in this world to help complete the big picture that God has designed for your life.

When your self-esteem gets low, remind yourself of who you were created to be.

You might say, "Well, all I do is this or that. I hardly even leave my house. I don't ever see anyone or talk to anyone." But you would be surprised at the people you have already impacted in your life.

I know people who are homebound and unable to leave their home, yet they're making an impact online or through their loved ones who go out into the world for them.

I can think of people I've seen or met through brief interactions who I will never forget because of something they said or did or how they helped me. They will probably never know the impact because I never got the chance to tell them.

It could be something you said, a smile you gave, a simple interaction with a stranger that influenced someone in a positive way. You may have said something that made someone think about something in a different way that led to a positive route for their life.

No one will ever be able to be you. Someone might try to walk like you, dress like you, or talk like you—but they will never be you. You are needed in this big, crazy world. You are making an impact, whether you know it or not.

So, continue to be yourself. You are a part of the big picture.

Be your own best cheerleader.

I have heard people say, *"I'm my own worst critic."* It's funny to hear people say that because no one likes to be criticized, yet we criticize ourselves on a regular basis.

If you criticize yourself on a regular basis, you may eventually start believing the criticism. Being excessively hard on yourself could lead to low self-esteem.

Instead of being your own worst critic, why not become your own cheerleader? Encourage yourself to be all God created you to be.

Sometimes it's easier to cheer others on when they're doing something great. When friends ask for our opinion of a new hairstyle or outfit, we often try to find something positive to say. Why not do the same for yourself? Focus on what you like about yourself.

Be your own cheerleader by believing the best about yourself. Believing the best about yourself means looking for the positive instead of pointing out the negative.

Being your own cheerleader means focusing on your positive qualities rather than feeling bad about your weaknesses.

There are people in your life who will always cheer you on, but why not start cheering yourself on? Pump yourself up to pursue your goals. Encourage yourself to do the thing you have always wanted to do.

Pick yourself up when you make mistakes. The past is in the past, and you cannot redo it. Focus on today and what you can do right now.

Being your own cheerleader means finding out who you are, what your strengths are, and what you have to offer the world. It means loving yourself, loving God, and loving others.

When you are your own best cheerleader—and you love the person God created you to be—it will be easy to love others.

Other people's opinion of you should not dictate your own opinion.

At some point, the internet became an automatic trusted expert on every single subject. There are people who make life decisions based on random sources.

While there are some credible sources of information on the internet, it's hard to determine what those sources are, especially in the age of artificial intelligence.

One of the monsters the internet has created is the boldness people have to make unkind comments on others' social media posts. People say things online that they would never say to someone's face.

In a world where everyone is looking for some type of validation, either in business or personal, it feels good to receive "likes" and positive feedback. But the danger in receiving public applause is that it can lead to a need for constant approval.

Your opinion of yourself or how you feel about yourself should not come from anyone but you. Yes, you will receive positive feedback that may be encouraging, but don't allow that feedback to guide your decisions or form your own view of yourself.

Do not allow others' opinions of you to dictate how you feel about yourself. Everyone is entitled to their own opinion. Most people see things from their own window of life. More than likely, their opinion of you stems from their personal experiences and biases.

If you know you have certain gifts and talents, use them. Continue to enhance your strengths and do what you enjoy. We all have areas we could work on and do better in. If someone criticizes you in one of those areas, don't let it bother you. Just continue to grow and enjoy what you do.

Walk in your own confidence. Don't be swayed by public opinion, especially when you know the truth.

God cares more about your heart than your outward appearance.

David is a well-known man in the Bible for various reasons, but one of the most memorable is his battle with a giant named Goliath.

Goliath had been tormenting David's family for a long time because no one could defeat him. But with God's strength and power, David was able to defeat Goliath with one smooth stone from his slingshot.

The crazy thing about this whole situation is that David was very young and was smaller than the other men who were afraid of Goliath. He was even too small to wear the armor the king provided for him to fight Goliath.

At another point in David's life, when he was being chosen as the new king, the existing king, King Saul, and the prophet Samuel looked at David's stature and felt he was too small. However, God let them know that He does not look on the outward appearance of men, He looks at our heart.

Knowing that the condition of my heart means more to God than my size motivates me to put more effort into refining what's inside me than improving how I look.

Do you spend more time putting on makeup or looking good than you do strengthening your inner self?

Based on David's story, God cares more about you building your faith internally than He does about your appearance.

Looking nice can help you feel good about yourself—and that's okay. But in the process of looking good on the outside, make sure you take care of your heart.

Take care of your heart by studying scriptures that build your faith, nurturing your relationship with God through prayer, surrounding yourself with positive people, practicing gratitude, and showing love and kindness to others.

Personal Reflection

What are the gifts and talents that I believe God has blessed me with?

What can I start doing to use my gifts and talents?

Love and embrace everything you were created to be while at the same time praying for God's help in the areas where you struggle.

Prayer for When Your Self-esteem is Low

Heavenly Father, thank You for creating me to be awesome.
When I am feeling doubtful of myself and my abilities, remind me of the gifts and
talents that You blessed me with.
Give me the courage to use my gifts and talents.
Remind me that my life is not about me, it's about helping others.
Nudge me when I am near someone who needs the unique gifts
You gave me to share.
Thank You for helping me to see You in me,
as I live my life from day to day. Amen.

Bible Verse for When Your Self-esteem is Low

Thank you for making me so wonderfully complex!
Your workmanship is marvelous—how well I know it.
Psalm 139:14

CHAPTER 5

When You Are Worried

Worrying will not accomplish anything.

I used to be the queen of worrying. I am one of those people who overthink every single thing.

People who analyze everything tend to worry more than others, because we are constantly thinking, planning, and analyzing everything and everybody.

But through many life experiences, I've learned that looking on the bright side of things instead of worrying helps lighten the load.

You can sit and think for hours, but overthinking will be completely useless. Worrying doesn't accomplish anything. It won't get you any further than you were before you started.

When you're sick, worrying won't heal your body. Worrying won't solve problems. Worrying won't fix a flat tire, and standing there thinking about it won't get you any closer to your destination.

The next time you find yourself worrying, try this:

- **Do something to lighten the load.** Start by saying a prayer specifically about the situation. It doesn't matter how small or impossible it may seem, praying takes the burden off you and places it in God's hands.

- **Replace fear with faith.** God will work everything out for your good.

- **Be open to God's answer.** Keep your heart, eyes, and ears open. The answer could come in the form of someone close to you, a perfect stranger, a Bible verse, a friend, or unforeseen outcomes. When you pray sincerely, God will answer.

Don't waste time worrying. There is no mental, physical, or spiritual benefit in it. Pray instead. Hope instead. Believe and trust God instead.

Turn your worries into prayers.

There have been many times in my life when I was worried about something or someone, but when I prayed, God turned things completely around. Sickness, children's well-being, parents, problems, and life in general can cause worry and fear. Through the years, I have learned to turn my worries into prayer—and it is very effective.

When you find yourself worrying, turn those worries into prayers. Problems will come, but when you pray about the things that trouble you, God hears your prayers and will move on your behalf.

When you worry about something, the thoughts will weigh you down and cause you to feel heavier with time. Using the time to pray about the situation will help you to feel lighter.

When you're facing a tough situation that you don't know how to handle, pause wherever you are and take a few minutes to pray about it. Pray for everyone involved in your tough situations. He can transform everyone involved and turn things completely around.

It only takes a little faith to pray. Just pray sincerely from your heart, and God will hear you. You might not receive the answer you want, but things will definitely turn out for your good.

God really cares about every single thing you go through. He loves you and He's always there to listen when you pray.

Turning your worries into prayers takes the burdens off your back and places them into God's hands. Worries and fears eventually become victories when you turn them into prayer.

We cannot change anything by worrying, but God can change everything when we pray.

Prayer should be your first response.

I once wondered why firetrucks are usually the first to arrive on the scene of an accident, until I found out that firefighters are "first responders."

First responders are people who are trained to respond to emergencies and provide aid at the scene. They're often the first to arrive and are critical to preparing for and responding to an incident.

Regardless of the situation, first responders work to ensure everyone on the scene has the best possible chance of survival.

In regard to first responses, what is your first response to drastic news?

Do you immediately pray when you hear bad news, or do you cry and worry and try to figure things out on your own?

The first response when passing a traffic accident on the highway should be to pray for those involved. When you see unhoused people on the street, your first response should be to pray for them.

When you hear about someone's downfall, the first thing you should do is pray for their restoration and strength. Consider the fact that it could be you in their place.

When you hear devastating news about someone's fatal illness diagnosis, you should immediately pray with compassion for their healing. Speak faith and hope for them to be healed through whatever treatment they are receiving and for a miracle.

To look on the bright side means to hope for the best for everyone, especially those facing hardship. Be a first responder to other people's misfortunes by praying for them and hoping for their best.

When we all pray for each other, those prayers will release God's power and love into our lives.

Hoping for the best brings light.

There is a bright side of life, even when darkness is all around. Brightness comes when you pray. There is a lot of darkness in the world these days. But when darkness comes your way, just keep praying, and God will give you the strength to make it through.

Sometimes life gets so dark that it feels heavy. You can feel the thickness of darkness in the air. If you ever feel that weight, say a prayer and hope for the best. And if the heaviness keeps coming back, just pray and pray again. Don't give up.

Darkness could come in a number of ways—a medical diagnosis, a lost child, a sick relative, a death in the family, or any other tragedy. Yet even in the midst of darkness, light is available to you.

Praying brings light. When you pray and ask God for strength, the Holy Spirit will empower you and lift you up out of despair, providing you with the courage you need to progress.

Hoping for the best brings light. When you continue to hope and believe that things will get better, they will get better. Hope shines light in a dark situation, just like a flashlight or candle lights up a room.

Remembering what God has done brings light. Your testimonies of God's goodness will propel you forward, helping you press through the pain and into greater blessings. When you think about all the wonderful things God has done for you before, your heart will be filled with joy and will push out the darkness.

Keep praying, hoping, and believing. Continue to remember the times God blessed you in the past. If He blessed you before, He is certainly able to bless you again.

Believing means you trust that something is already done. When you pray, believe that God already has the answer.

Keep praying. Keep hoping. Keep remembering. Keep believing.

Prayer is your lifeline to God.

Plants require proper soil, water, and sunshine to be able to sustain and grow. Just like plants, we need the proper soil of God's Word to grow.

God is your life's source. He created you, and staying connected to Him ensures your survival.

Staying in touch with God allows Him to water and feed you through reading the Bible, through the positive things you take in daily, through an encouraging word from a friend, and even through other unexpected sources.

A crisis can strike at any time, but you will be prepared to stand strong when you have built yourself up with prayer. You may be caught off guard at times, but God never is. He knows every phase of your life and is right there with you to see you through.

When you pray, the Holy Spirit intercedes (or pleads) to God on your behalf, letting Him know exactly what you need. Sometimes, you may not know what to say when you pray, but the Holy Spirit tells God exactly what you need.

The Holy Spirit also refreshes you when you pray, just like water refreshes plants. There is so much strength in prayer. Even the worst situation feels lighter when you stop and pray about it.

Prayer connects you with your lifeline and source of your life—God.

The more you communicate with your lifeline, the more you will be able to recognize God's voice leading and guiding you. Knowing God's voice is like having dinner with a friend in a crowded restaurant. You hear all of the voices around you, but you know your friend's voice because you have heard it so often.

At times you just don't feel like praying, but if you take some time to say a few words, even if it's "Help me, Lord" or "Thank you, Jesus," you will store up strength you will need later for difficult situations.

Stay in touch with your lifeline. Pray always. Always pray.

Make peace of mind your priority.

We live in a busy world full of internet craziness, social media rants, economic instability, violence, and even dark entertainment from a variety of sources.

There is so much going on around us, it sometimes gets hard to live in peace without the interruption of bad news.

When you start to feel fearful or overwhelmed with life, it's time to take action to prioritize your peace.

Take these steps to prioritize your peace:

- **Clear your space of the things that are mentally troubling or emotionally overwhelming.** Offer a loving "no" when asked to do things that would overcrowd your space. This will free up time you can use for activities that relax your mind.

- **Examine your daily activities and remove those that do not fulfill your heart's desire.**

Sometimes children can be enrolled in too many extracurricular activities that can overcrowd your time and make you feel overwhelmed.

If you have young children, consider these questions to help determine which activities are necessary:

- Is the activity required for academic success?

- Is your child fully engaged in the activity, and does it build confidence?

- Can your child still enjoy family time alongside the activity?

- Does the activity help develop new skills or enhance personal growth?

If your answer is "no" to any of these questions, the activity may not be contributing to the child's personal growth and is counterproductive.

Consider removing those things that are not aligned with your personality and living your true self. This will free up some time for you and will allow you to live with more purpose, freedom, and peace.

Analyze your rest time and take steps to make sure you get enough rest. Sometimes a good nap can completely refresh your well-being and relieve the frequency of anxiety episodes.

Of all the activities you participate in, make sure you prioritize your peace of mind. **Don't let anything or anyone compromise your mental and physical well-being.**

God can handle any problem you have.

Mental health is just as important as physical health. One of the things that can keep your mind strong is not allowing worry to consume your thoughts. Overthinkers have the hardest time with not worrying because we tend to analyze every little thing.

It's okay to try to piece things together, but at some point, you have to give your brain time to recharge. Give your brain a break by giving your problems to God—pray about it, do what you can, and then free your mind. Try your best not to worry. When you worry, your brain is working overtime and is not recharging.

The next time you find yourself worrying, try this:

1. Picture yourself holding the problem in your hand and then handing it over to God.

2. Once you hand the problem over to God, do not think about it.

3. If you find yourself taking the problem back and worrying, just hand it right back to God.

Situations will arise over and over throughout life. But the bright side is that the more problems we have, the more practice we get with prayer. And the more practice we get with prayer, the more we experience the goodness of God through answered prayers.

Take care of your mind by giving your burdens to God through prayer. When worrying tries to tackle your mind, say a prayer. When you can't help but try to figure things out, say a prayer. Trust God. He can handle any problem you have.

God will work everything out for your good. When you least expect it, things will get better than they were before. Say a prayer, have faith, and try not to worry.

Watch what you eat.

There is an old cliché that says, "What goes in must come out." While this quote refers to the food we eat, the same principle is true regarding what you feed your mind and spirit. When you feed your mind and spirit with positivity, you will reap positivity and spiritual maturity. Your body tells you when you eat something that does not digest well—it's an uncomfortable feeling. The same is true for your mind and spirit.

Listen to yourself when something feels wrong. Be intentional with filtering your mental and spiritual intake. Be selective about what you eat mentally, physically, and spiritually. **Try the following ideas to watch what you feed your mind and spirit:**

- **Pay attention to how you feel while reading, watching, or listening to something.** Do you feel like you are being lifted? Or do you feel uncomfortable like something is bothering you?

- **Does what you are taking in strengthen your faith?** Or does it send you into a state of depression?

Whatever you feed your mind should be positive and should sustain your peace of mind. Be sure to feed your spirit with prayer, scriptures, and whatever strengthens you spiritually so that you will stay connected to God who created you. Sometimes, due to your environment, you may not have a choice of what you hear or see. In those situations, don't allow negativity to compromise your peace of mind or your spiritual strength. It's okay to walk away from situations that are negatively affecting you.

Keep your mind on positive things and a prayer in your heart. Feeding yourself with positive things will help you look on the bright side of any situation you will face.

Personal Reflection

What can I do instead of worrying when I have a problem?

Prayer for When You Are Worried

Heavenly Father, sometimes I can't help but worry about
family, situations, work, and other things.
Lord, help me to put my trust in You.
I know that You will make everything alright.
I put my hand in Your hand and ask You to lead the way.
Take away all worry.
I put my faith and confidence in You that You will work out every situation that
I am worried about.
There is nothing too hard for You.
Thank You, God, for peace of mind. Amen.

Bible Verse for When You Are Worried

Give all your worries and cares to God, for he cares about you.
1 Peter 5:7

Chapter 6

When You Are Anxious

God cares about the little things.

On New Year's Eve, our dogs, Chloe and Milo, broke out of our backyard, frightened by the fireworks. We were away on vacation and didn't find out they had escaped until we returned home.

I love my dogs and was heartbroken that they were gone. I prayed that God would help them find their way home or help us find them. We put up posters in the neighborhoods nearby and posted online. We also visited the animal shelter daily looking for them.

We found Milo a few days into the new year, but six weeks passed before we found Chloe. It was on Valentines Day when we received a phone call from a woman. She thought she saw Chloe hanging around a small pond in her neighborhood.

We went to the pond, and sure enough, Chloe was there. I believe with all my heart it was God who blessed our dogs to return home. God cares about the little things in our lives that we care about, no matter how small. God knew my heart was hurting. He heard my prayer and brought Chloe and Milo back home safely.

God cares so much for you that nothing is too little or too big for Him to do for you. If it matters to you, it matters to Him.

You might feel like you are overreacting to a tough situation in your life or making a big deal out of nothing. Well, if it matters to you, it matters to God. You are not overreacting. You are acting out of concern for things to turn out right. God cares about what you care about.

God will always take care of you and do what is best for you. Take all your cares to God. It doesn't matter how small or how big you think the problem is. God can handle it. He loves you and cares about every little thing in your life.

Change the channel in your mind.

When anxiety tries to take you down and paralyze you, fight back by changing the channel in your mind. Thoughts can create fear and anxiety in your brain and turn into terrible "movies." Then, anxiety triggers panic and increased heart rate.

But when anxiety attacks, change the channel in your mind and you'll slowly see a difference. Imagine yourself switching the channel of negative thoughts to a channel filled with positive thoughts. Your thoughts will make things seem much worse than they really are. The things you're telling yourself may or may not be true.

Thoughts can cause you to falsely accuse people. Anxiety can lead you to doubt yourself, especially in areas you're greatly talented in. **The next time you are feeling anxious, try this:**

- Take a deep breath and redirect your thoughts to something positive. Reflect on a Bible verse such as "I can do all things through Christ who strengthens me."

- Change the image of yourself to the potential you know you have inside. Focus on your positive qualities.

- Assume the best about others. Maybe they're not trying to hurt you. Maybe what's happening is completely honest on their part.

- Look for the good in your current situation. Mentally walk through a list of pros about everyone and everything involved. What are the pros you can see that are real?

When you change your perspective, you will feel better and will be able to move forward. In the big picture of things, everything will be all right.

Steps to calm your spirit during anxiety.

Anxiety is the opposite of calmness and reassurance. People experience anxiety for a variety of reasons. Unfortunately, it is a genuine experience that attacks a lot of people.

There was a king in the Bible who at times would become deeply troubled in his spirit. He was probably experiencing anxiety attacks. The king would call for David, who was only a shepherd at the time, to play his musical instrument for him when he was troubled. When David played, the king's troubled spirit would settle.

Sometimes when we are troubled, it means that our spiritual core is being shaken. This may be caused by worried thoughts, relationship conflict, or bad news. Whatever the reason for the anxiety, you can calm your spirit by connecting with the sweet presence of God.

Try these steps to calm your spirit when you experience anxiety:

1. Find a quiet place where you can be still for a few minutes.

2. Take a deep breath. Anxiety often causes you to lose oxygen to your brain, which is why you might feel weak in your knees. Taking a deep breath releases fresh air to your brain and replenishes you.

3. Ask God to help you and quiet your troubled mind. Saying a prayer in the middle of the anxiety will take the pressure off you and build your confidence in God.

4. Imagine placing your hand in God's hand, letting Him lead you and take care of you.

5. Move forward in confidence, knowing that everything will be alright.

It's okay to laugh at yourself.

I stood up and followed the line of people to the table at the front of the church to give my offering. I was eight years old, and my mom had handed me money to give on her behalf. I walked to the table and placed the money in the basket.

When I turned around to return to my seat, there were some children sitting in a nearby pew pointing and laughing hysterically at me. I was horrified, hurt, and confused. Why were they laughing at me?

When I sat down, my mom pulled the white handkerchief off the top of my head—I had placed it there before walking to the front. I then realized the children were laughing at something silly I had intentionally done, and I laughed too.

It's amazing how much lighter problems can seem when we learn to laugh at ourselves. Not taking yourself too seriously can make a huge difference to your self-esteem.

Most people are too worried about their own image to spend time thinking about yours. The next time you are nervous—whether it's a job interview, doing a good job at work, or giving a public presentation—try not to take yourself too seriously. Take a deep breath, release all tension, and focus on the great opportunity ahead of you.

So, what if something happens to embarrass you? It will not be the worst thing that could happen to you—it didn't kill you. Don't overthink the situation. Assume the best of everything and everybody. It is never as bad as you think it is.

Free your mind from worrying about things you cannot control. Remove all self-doubt from your mind. Believe in yourself. Cheer yourself on. Remind yourself of how impressed you are with how far you have come.

The next time you are feeling nervous, smile and ask yourself, "Am I overthinking this?" "Am I taking it too seriously?"

All is well.

There's a story in the Bible about a Shunammite woman whose son dies in her arms. She leaves home and runs to see the prophet Elisha to tell him about her son.

Before she reached the prophet, she saw family members who asked her how she was doing. She answered with, "All is well."

When she got closer to the prophet's location, one of the prophet's assistants asked her how she was doing. She responded with, *"All is well."*

I am sure the grieving mother was in terrible distress, but she responded to everyone's inquiry with a positive answer. Why would she respond this way when her son had just died?

I believe she spoke these words because she was praying and believing for a miracle for her son. She didn't want to waste time explaining her faith to anyone.

The heartbroken mom was focused on getting to the prophet who would more than likely pray for her or give her some encouraging words.

It takes courage to speak positive words when you are experiencing something horrible, especially when you don't see any help in sight.

Sometimes you are hurting, and you want people to know, but you don't know what to say or who you can trust. Sometimes you need compassion when you are suffering, but you don't know who to go to.

God cares when we are suffering. God is with you and is working everything out. When you don't know who to talk to, just speak the words "All is well" in faith, knowing that God is working everything out.

Speaking positive words when you are experiencing a trial will help increase your faith and give you strength to move forward.

No matter what you are going through, all is well.

Personal Reflection

What can I tell myself to feel calm when anxiety sets in?

Prayer for When You Are Anxious

Heavenly Father, I am feeling anxiety right now.
I am in constant fear, dread, and uneasiness.
Sometimes the anxiety gets in the way of me doing my schoolwork, working, or going out into the world.
Lord, anxiety is a "thorn in my flesh" that does not seem to go away. It is an annoyance, a source of agony, and it hinders my progress at times.
Please help me to be calm and peaceful.
Help me to walk in complete confidence and
faith in You and who You created me to be.
Give me the strength and courage
to do the things I need to do until this goes away.
Thank you, God. Amen.

Bible Verse for When You Are Anxious

When anxiety was great within me, your consolation brought me joy.

Psalm 94:19

CHAPTER 7

When You Are Afraid

You can do whatever you set your mind to do.

As I climbed the wet rocks with water flowing down from the top of the mountain, I was terrified. I had reluctantly agreed to climb the mountain with my husband.

What was I thinking? The rocks were so wet and slippery. I don't even think I wore the right type of shoes for mountain climbing. I asked myself, "What if I fall? What if the rope holding us breaks?" Still, I followed my husband up the mountain, holding tightly onto the rope, while he pulled me up each rock when I needed help.

Once I reached the top of the mountain, I was so relieved and thankful to be alive. Now, we were headed to the zip line. I was fully committed. There was no turning back at that point. The zip line worker secured me, and off I went flying over trees and waterways.

When I landed at the end of the zip line, I was so proud of myself for pushing through fear. Facing my fear of mountain climbing and zip lining gave me courage.

With God on your side, you can push through any fearful situation in your life. Even though you might be terrified, God is right there watching over you.

Sometimes in life, you have to take risks. You may have to climb some mountains before you can zip line through the beautiful scenery of life. But you can do whatever you set your mind to. God is right there with you when you try new things and even when you take crazy risks. God will lift you up and push you through when you feel like you can't make it.

So, don't put limits on yourself or on God. Push through the fear and God will help you through. You will come out on the other side full of courage for the next thing you set your mind to do.

You will always rise to the top.

I learned how to swim when I was 50 years old. I had several swimming classes over the years, but I could never get over my fear of the water enough to learn the techniques.

When I turned forty-nine, I registered for swimming classes. I was fortunate to have a great swim instructor. By the end of the semester, I was finally swimming. **I learned several life lessons during those weeks of swimming classes:**

Sometimes you have to face your fears head-on. During the first week of class, the instructor told us to place our face under the water in the shallow end of the pool. The purpose was to get rid of the fear of the water—and it worked.

Trust the teacher. Just as I had to trust my swimming instructor to protect me when I learned the progressive techniques, I have to trust that God will protect me through life. The longer we live, the more lessons we will have to learn. The bright side of all the lessons and tests is that we graduate to a higher level when we finally learn. When we finally get it, we can move on to higher heights and deeper depths.

If you ever hit rock bottom, you will rise to the top. During the final week of swimming class, the instructor asked us to sit on the bottom of the deep end of the pool. When I dived in and tried to sit on the floor of the pool, my body would not stay down. Regardless of how hard I tried, I kept rising to the top of the water. This is the epiphany that removed all fear of the water for me and taught me that nothing could ever hold me down. There is no problem in life that could ever keep you down. With God on your side, you will always rise to the top.

So, don't let fear stop you from reaching your goals. **Push through, and even though you might fall or hit bottom at times, you will always rise to the top.** You have the best teacher you could ever have when you put your trust in Jesus.

Fear can fuel your progress.

Fighting or running away are natural responses to stress. A stressful situation can cause your heart to beat quickly and could even affect your breathing. It could make your legs feel weak as if you'll faint. When this happens, there is also adrenaline running through your bloodstream. This adrenaline is the body's way of supplying energy to all parts of your body. You can either use that adrenaline to your advantage or you can try to suppress it.

The next time you're getting ready to give a presentation, start a new project, or do a job interview, and you feel weak in your knees because you are so nervous, use the fear adrenaline to fuel your actions.

The next time something terrifies you, try this:

- Take a deep breath. Slow down. Think about your next move. Don't suppress the adrenaline.

- Use fear to push out your words. Use fear to energize your voice and your movement.

- Don't worry about people seeing your nervousness. They will never know you're nervous when you push through it.

Don't give in to fear. Use fear to your advantage and allow it to energize you.

You're in the right place at the right time. This moment was meant for you to shine. Don't let fear dull your moment or steal it away from you. Take advantage of this chance and shine your light.

Be your authentic self. No one can do this the way you can, so be yourself.

Let your true personality show with no inhibitions. Don't let fear hold you back. You have greatness inside of you. Let it out. Let your light shine.

Personal Reflection

What can I do to be bold and courageous when I am afraid?

Prayer for When You Are Afraid

Heavenly Father, I lay all my cares and fears before You.
You have always watched over me. Help me now in this situation.
Help me to put my trust in You.
You protected the three Hebrew boys when they were thrown into a fire.
You kept Daniel safe in the den of lions. You kept David safe when his enemies
chased him to kill him.
I have been in dangerous situations before, and You protected me.
I ask that You do that again.
Please remove all fear from my heart as You send
Your angels of protection to keep me from harm.
Thank You, God. Amen.

Bible Verse for When You are Afraid

> Even when I walk through the darkest valley,
> I will not be afraid, for you are close beside me.
> Your rod and your staff protect and comfort me.
> Psalm 23:4

CHAPTER 8

When You Are Confused

Does the choice align with your life purpose?

Many times, confusion comes when we have too many life activities. It gets hard to see the way when the road is clouded with too many things.

Consider these questions to help you align your choices with your life purpose:

- **Does the choice you're considering align with your values and priorities?** Your personal values and priorities will help you stay committed and energized when you feel like giving up.

- **Will you be able to use your gifts and talents?** Make sure your choice is something that will allow you to use your gifts and talents either now or in the future. You feel most alive and passionate about life when you're doing what you were created for.

- **Will the choice you are considering allow you to help the people you are drawn to help?** You should be able to connect with the people you are drawn to help either directly or indirectly, in some capacity, at some point.

When you are being pulled in different directions, take the road that allows you to be the true person God created you to be.

Don't let anyone pressure you into making a decision. Ask for time to think it over and sleep on it. Sleep can clear your mind and improve your thoughts. If you compromise your life purpose, then you may also compromise the energy you need to accomplish your goals, potentially slowing down your progress.

Make the best decision you can in that moment. Align your goals and decisions with your life purpose and you will prosper in every way.

Sometimes you have to clear out the gutter.

House gutters collect rainwater from the edge of a roof, channel it through a trench, direct the water down through pipes, and then pour the water away from the house's foundation. This process helps prevent water damage to the roof.

In life, when you are confused and don't know what to do, you may need to clean out your "gutter." The gutter can represent a cluttered mind, overwhelmed by too much on your plate.

Ask yourself these questions to identify activities to clear from your "gutter":

- Do my current activities align with who I really am?

- What are my goals, and will this activity help me accomplish them?

- Is this activity something I can afford to invest my time and money in?

- Have I prayed about this activity, and do I feel at peace with moving forward?

If you answered "no" to any of these questions, there may be some things you need to remove from your gutter. Reflect on the questions you answered "no" to and consider ways you might let go of the excess or make meaningful changes. Take time to clean out the gutter and remove anything that is wasting your time.

Times goes by quickly. Don't waste it doing things that have no value. When you spend time doing things that align with your values and your life purpose, there is no waste of time.

Don't feel pressured to spend time doing something that you know hinders progress toward your goals.

Let the Spirit lead you.

Ultimately, God has a plan for your life and already knows your path. When you pray and ask Him, He will lead and guide you along the way that is meant for you.

I like to think of it as a father with his children. A father wants what is best for his children. When there is something his children want that makes them happy, it also makes their father happy—so long as it doesn't hurt them.

Maybe you're not sure if what you want is in God's will. Just as a father wants what is best for his children, God wants what is best for you. Pray about the choices you have and then make the best decision you can.

God will work everything together for your good, regardless of the decisions you make.

There have been times in my life when I made decisions and plans, but they were completely changed according to God's will. I remember one particular instance when I bought a plane ticket to visit someone, but during the layover, the person cancelled. I ended up staying at the layover location to help a family member with something important—something I hadn't even known they needed help with.

Making decisions and plans are a normal part of life. Some decisions are easy, while others are difficult to make because we don't know how things will turn out.

The good news is that when Jesus left this earth, He left the Holy Spirit with us to lead, guide, and comfort us in times of uncertainty. When we put our faith in Christ and allow the Holy Spirit to guide us, we can accomplish great things.

To put it simply, the Holy Spirit is like your intuition or gut feeling, but far more powerful. The Holy Spirit is your divine guidance. Have you ever started to do something and had a gut feeling telling you not to? Have you ever had a strong feeling about someone, but you didn't know why?

The Holy Spirit leads us in a similar but more powerful way. He leads us in alignment, or according to God's will for our life. He gives us discernment or sensitivity to watch out for pitfalls.

Spend time in prayer, talking to God, and you will get to know His voice that speaks to you through the Holy Spirit. It is the most powerful way to receive guidance for your life decisions.

Personal Reflection

What personal values and priorities will I base my major decisions on when I am confused?

Prayer for When You are Confused

Heavenly Father, I pray that You will remove all confusion and give me a clear mind. Remove any thoughts and doubts that are clouding my mind. If there are any desires in my heart that are not suitable for me, I ask You to remove them.
Give me clarity of heart, mind, and soul.
Help me to focus only on the things that align with Your will and plan for my life.
Thank You for sending Your Holy Spirit to guide me.
Help me to hear Your voice and give me the strength to obey Your will. Amen.

Bible Verse for When You are Confused

Trust in the Lord with all your heart; do not depend on your own understanding. Seek his will in all you do, and he will show you which path to take.

Proverbs 3:5-6

CHAPTER 9

When It's Hard to Forgive

God forgives us, so we should forgive others.

There was a time when someone betrayed me, and it hit me hard. For months, I felt angry and deeply hurt because of what they had done. I prayed for God to remove the anger and malice I was feeling. I also prayed for the people involved, that God would change whatever caused them to do what they did to me and others.

When I sincerely prayed with all my heart for God to help me, something wonderful happened. God replaced the anger I had with love. Not only did I begin to feel love for those involved, but I also had compassion for their struggles.

The more I prayed about the situation, the more I saw the situation in a whole new light. I was able to put myself in their shoes and understand why they had done what they did to betray me. Although what they did was still wrong, I gained compassion for them through prayer, which helped me see things from their perspective.

God replaced the anger I had with love and peace. He lovingly reminded me of the times He forgave me for similar things I had done in the past and should, therefore, forgive others. As I reflected on God's love and forgiveness towards me, I couldn't help but walk in love and forgiveness for those who wronged me.

Even though they never took full responsibility for what happened, I forgive them because God forgave me. I love them because God loves me.

God's love for you is so great, it can help you love others in times of betrayal. His love can transform your unforgiving heart into a forgiving heart, even if the other person does not express remorse.

Forgiveness may take time, but you will eventually get there. One day, you will realize that you must let go of the anger before it consumes you.

God forgives us when we do wrong because of His loving mercy. Pray and ask Him to help you show mercy to those who betrayed you.

Forgiveness takes time, but it is possible.

Forgiving someone is easier said than done—but you can do it. It takes time, but eventually, you will be able to forgive.

True forgiveness is about loving God for forgiving you, loving yourself enough to release unforgiveness and bitterness, and loving those who have hurt you, even if they never express remorse.

To be able to forgive, you must look forward. When feelings of anger hit you, keep looking ahead. Don't look back. You will have good days and bad days. There will be moments when you will change your mind about forgiving. You've been hurt, betrayed, and have a right to be angry.

Moving forward may mean taking a break from the person who hurt you while both of you get help dealing with the violation of trust. This break may be especially necessary if the situation involved any form of abuse.

Some people may act as if they don't even care that they've hurt you. This cavalier behavior frustrates you even more. But whether they apologize and show remorse or not, take control of your peace of mind and move forward.

If you hold on to anger, resentment, or bitterness, you will carry the emotional weight like baggage—dragging through life slowly, with heaviness. Take the time you need to release the hurtful emotions you are experiencing. Give yourself permission to grieve the relationship that has been broken.

Give yourself the space needed to heal. Sometimes, this means loving people from a distance. Forgiveness means moving forward and doing what is best for your own personal peace of mind. And your peace of mind is a critical part of your well-being.

Take all the time you need to move into forgiveness. It will happen.

Forgiveness is for you, not for the other person.

You are the main person who benefits when you forgive someone, because you are freeing your mind from bitterness and resentment. Don't let unforgiveness keep you from doing what you were born to do. Release the feelings of anger and resentment and replace them with love and compassion for yourself.

I know it's not easy to forgive, especially when the person who hurt you is someone close. It's hard, but you have to move past trying to figure out why they betrayed you.

Here are a few personal benefits of forgiving someone:

- You free yourself to live life with no inhibitions.

- You welcome healing and peace into your heart, allowing yourself to walk in freedom to pursue your purpose.

- You can walk in happiness without the chains of bitterness and resentment.

- You prevent anger from festering, which can take a toll on your physical health.

When you hold on to anger, you're only hurting yourself. Focus on taking care of your well-being. Pray and ask God to heal your hurting heart and for the strength to move forward. Letting go of the pain is easier said than done, but you can do it. In time, you'll be able to look at the person who hurt you and feel no anger.

Forgiveness means moving forward and doing what is best for your own peace of mind. It may be one of the hardest things you'll do in life, but it's necessary for your personal growth.

What if they do not apologize?

Some people will never apologize for hurting you. Even when they do, they may not show the level of remorse you believe they should.

For your own peace of mind, you must forgive the person who betrayed you, whether they apologize or not. I am not saying you should condone what they did. Your pain and anger are valid, and you have the right to be treated with kindness. But if they refuse to take responsibility for their actions, you must take charge of your own healing and peace of mind.

Having expectations for their remorse could lead to more disappointment for you. Your act of forgiveness and their act of recompense (making up for what they did) should not be interdependent. Hopefully, they will sincerely apologize and be willing to make amends for the wrong they did, but if they don't, make the decision to truly forgive, and then take all the time you need to resolve the pain within yourself. It could take years to rebuild your trust and release the anger.

If someone is not willing to apologize on any level, they are showing you they don't see anything wrong with what they did. And if they don't see anything wrong with what they did, they are likely to repeat the behavior. Ask yourself, *Is this the type of repeated behavior I want in my life? Is this behavior helpful or harmful to me?*

It's easier to forgive than it is to forget, but even if you never forget, you can still move on without bringing it up again. When you forgive and move on without talking about it, you release yourself from the pain of reliving it over and over. You also clear the way for you to move on and focus on the things you need to do in your daily life.

When people refuse to apologize for hurting you, be kind to yourself by not worrying about the situation. Make plans to move forward without pain and anger in your life.

Don't believe the negative hype.

Have you ever watched a movie where one of the characters has flashbacks? The flashback interrupts the scene and takes you back to an earlier moment. You might have flashbacks when someone hurts you and you have decided to forgive them. Like flashbacks in a movie, your mind will start replaying past moments when that person hurt you. The mental flashbacks can hype you up with thoughts about the person that might not even be true. Your mind will build propaganda against the person who wronged you, pushing you further into anger.

The flashbacks of negative thoughts come on fast and strong when you are trying to forgive someone. So many questions pop in your head, beating you down with feelings of betrayal and confusion. *Why did they do it? Was it my fault? How did I miss it? What could I have done to prevent it?*

If you have decided to move forward with the person who wronged you and forgive them for what they did, you will have to block the flashbacks. Don't believe the negative hype that the flashbacks are causing.

You'll never be able to control what somebody else does. For that reason, the betrayal you experienced is not your fault. That person made the decision.

You're responsible for your choices only. Remove the burden of trying to figure out what you could've done differently to prevent what they did. Focus on what can be done in the future to live in peace and strengthen the relationship.

If you have decided to stay in the relationship, then don't look back. Don't believe the hype or the flashbacks of doubtful thoughts. Move forward with love and patience—for yourself and for the person who betrayed you, who is hopefully working to rebuild your trust.

Let mercy lead the way as you rebuild, one day at a time.

Forgiveness sometimes means loving someone from a distance.

Although forgiveness is critical for your own peace of mind, it doesn't mean you should subject yourself to repeated abuse. In some circumstances, it's best to create space around you for your safety and well-being.

Just as you would protect a wound from getting scratched, you must protect your heart by covering it with wisdom and discernment.

Take these steps to create a safe space for yourself as you heal from verbal, emotional, or physical abuse:

- Prioritize your healing and listen to your intuition regarding the person who betrayed you.

- Place emotional and physical distance between you and them while they get the help they need.

- Avoid influences—people, events, situations, locations—that could potentially cause further harm to you.

- Set clear boundaries to protect your security, safety, and welfare.

Forgiveness doesn't mean giving permission for someone to keep causing harm. If you allow repeated abuse, you will never have the peace of mind you desire. You may still love the person who abused you, but placing distance would help you to heal and move forward.

Allow yourself to heal and forgive by making room for your safety and wellbeing. It may take a while for you to trust again, but don't give up. In time, you will walk in peace.

Personal Reflection

What will I remind myself of when I have a hard time forgiving someone?

Prayer for When It's Hard to Forgive

Heavenly Father, I ask that You give me a forgiving heart for this person. Lord, You know them better than I do, and You love them as much as You love me. Help me to love them, too. Help me to be kind and compassionate towards them. Lord, You forgave me of my sins, and I am so grateful. You don't hold any of my sins against me. Help me to forgive others who have wronged me. Remove any hatred I have in my heart towards them.

Take away any desire for vengeance. Even though they may never apologize, help me to forgive them like You forgave me. Have mercy on me, oh Lord, as I work through these feelings. Thank You, God. Amen.

Bible Verse for When It's Hard to Forgive

Get rid of all bitterness, rage, anger, harsh words, and slander, as well as all types of evil behavior. Instead, be kind to each other, tenderhearted, forgiving one another, just as God through Christ has forgiven you.
Ephesians 4:31-32

CHAPTER 10

When It's Hard to Forgive Yourself

There is only one perfect person who ever existed.

We all have a story. From birth to where we are right now, we're bound to make mistakes or bad choices.

I cringe when I think about some of the things I've done in my lifetime. Maybe you've made mistakes in your life. The reality is, they won't be the last. They may not be the same mistakes—or maybe they will. Either way, you must forgive yourself and ask for God's help to move forward. There is only one perfect person who ever existed, and that person is Jesus Christ.

One of the many reasons I love the Bible is because it's full of stories about people who made mistakes but were still used by God. David committed adultery and murder. Samson was a womanizer. Rahab was a prostitute. Jonah ran from God. Peter denied Jesus three times. Paul persecuted Christians.

These are stories of redemption that remind us how merciful and loving God is. God loves us not because of who we are or what we do. He loves us because He is God. He is the very essence of forgiveness.

God is not like people who have a hard time forgetting the wrong you've done. He is full of compassion and grace, giving you the strength to get up and keep moving when you fall.

Receive God's mercy and forgiveness in your life. Walk in the freedom of His love for you. When you make mistakes, talk to God about them. If you struggle with something, ask for His help, and He will help you. He already knows your struggle and wants to help you.

When you find yourself beating yourself up over something you said or did, remind yourself that God loves you just the way you are. After all, He created you.

Don't let the past mistakes dictate your future. Receive God's mercy and forgiveness and walk the path to renewal.

Your father does not hold grudges.

There is no greater story of love and forgiveness than the parable of the prodigal son. In this story, a son asks his father for his inheritance. The son then wastes his inheritance and eventually becomes homeless and destitute.

He returns home, begs forgiveness from his father, and asks to be a servant. But instead of making his son a servant, the father welcomes him back into the family and throws a big party for him to celebrate his return home.

Just like the prodigal son's father, God never shames you. He corrects you with love, but He never condemns you. God's love for you is unconditional.

True forgiveness can only come from God. Without His grace and mercy, we have neither the power nor the authority to forgive. But when we are able to accept God's forgiveness for our sins, we will be able to forgive ourselves.

When we experience God's love and understand how He gave His only son, Jesus, for our sins, then we will be able to forgive ourselves.

When Jesus died on the cross, He prayed, "Father, forgive them." He did this while they were physically nailing him to the cross. Now, that's forgiveness!

God forgave us while we were still living in sin. When we take the time to sincerely pray and ask for forgiveness, He is merciful and will forgive us. He is not going to look at us and laugh and call us names and tell us we are unworthy. He is going to look at our heart and our sincerity and welcome us back home.

Just like the prodigal son's father, God is your Heavenly Father and He wants what is best for you. God wants you to walk in the freedom of His forgiveness.

God loves you, so you should love you. God sees the best in you, so you should see the best in you.

Don't worry about what people say or think about you or the mistakes you've made. Forgive yourself and walk in the freedom of God's love.

God loves you no matter what.

Whatever you do, do not condemn yourself to eternal judgment when you mess up. There is nothing you can do—or not do—to earn God's salvation. Salvation is a gift.

A gift is not something you have to earn or pay for. A gift is something that is freely given to you when you receive it. It's dangerous to think that you can earn God's love or His gift of salvation. If you were to think you could earn His love, you'd be trying every day to do that. Trying to earn God's love would be exhausting and disappointing because His love cannot be earned.

God loves you no matter what.

Just as a father loves his children with unconditional love, God loves you even when you do wrong. God's mercy spares you from punishment when you do wrong.

God is infinitely compassionate and always willing to forgive you. Even when you feel you deserve punishment, God's mercy will protect you. God loves you and forgives you when you need it most.

You've messed up before, and you will mess up again. Mistakes are part of the growing process. God knows you aren't perfect. Don't beat yourself into the ground when you misstep.

When you do slip, say a prayer and ask God for forgiveness. Ask Him for the strength to do better. He will forgive you every single time and will be there to help you when you ask. There is nowhere you can go that God will not be there waiting for you to reach out to Him.

Your life is not hopeless. You are not condemned. You're free to live in the grace of God through his strength and the mercy of his forgiveness when you ask Him.

Invite Jesus into your heart. Become His child. He loves His children unconditionally, no matter what.

Personal Reflection

What will I say to support myself when it is hard to forgive myself?

Prayer for When It's Hard to Forgive Yourself

Heavenly Father, thank you for loving me and forgiving me for all the wrong I've ever done and will ever do. Thank you for coming into my heart.
Thank You for seeing nothing but love when You look at me.
Help me to see myself the same way.
You see my heart and my desire to please You.
You don't even remember the ugly things I did because they are completely covered by Your love and the blood that You shed on the cross for me.
You know me as if I am Your own child because I am. You knew I would fall, and You were there to pick me up every time.
You love me with an extreme and passionate love and would never hold anything I have done against me.
Help me to forgive myself and to love myself and to move forward into the life of freedom that You have for me.
I am forgiven. I am free. There is no looking back. Amen.

Bible Verse for When It's Hard to Forgive Yourself

So now there is no condemnation for those who belong to Christ Jesus.

Romans 8:1

CHAPTER 11

When You Are Mourning

You will get through this.

One of my bonus daughters—my husband's cherished child—passed during the Covid pandemic, though not from Covid itself. During the Covid quarantine, schools, churches, beauty salons, and other public places were closed, leaving us isolated in our grief.

My husband fell into deep depression, emotionally and socially paralyzed by sorrow. My heart ached not only for him but for the loss of a bright light in our lives—a girl with so much personality and love for others.

I tried all I could to pull my husband out of the hole of sadness, but grief cannot be rushed. Despite his grief, he remained devoted to his family, just as I remained devoted to him—and to honoring her memory.

Grieving leaves a permanent hole in your heart for your loved one. I have witnessed grieving people with a blank gaze in their eyes, forced to face the world before they were ready. It's easy to become trapped in sorrow, struggling to find joy again.

Some marriages don't survive the loss of a child. The weight of grief, anger, and silence can tear people apart.

Thankfully, through prayer, love, kindness, patience, and therapy, my husband eventually emerged from his despair. He acknowledges he will never be the same but has found joy in life again. He sings, dances, and gardens like he used to, and his eyes gleam again.

You too can move forward while grieving. Take the time you need to mourn. Hold tight to the memories—the laughter, the love, the moments that made your loved one irreplaceable.

With time, patience, and unwavering love, you will get through this along with everyone else in your family.

God can replace your sorrow with joy.

My husband and I had just finished dinner at my mother-in-law's house at Christmas time when my phone rang. The call was from our neighbor's wife giving us the horrible news that her husband, our good friend, had just passed away. He had been diagnosed with a terminal illness less than a year earlier.

It was shocking to hear this news. We had prayed so hard for him, as if he were our own brother. We fervently asked God daily to heal him from that horrible disease. We were heartbroken and confused to learn that he passed away.

Days later, when we attended his memorial service, my heartache was quickly lifted as I listened to all his schoolmates speak about him. They talked endlessly about the wonderful things he had done—how he helped others and how he gave so fearlessly.

As I sat there listening to all his accolades, I couldn't help but be grateful for having ever known such a person. The grief I felt was replaced with joy in knowing that our friend would surely live in eternal peace with God. Hearing all those stories about him made me feel as if he had never left. The impression he left on all of us is still with us.

Treasure the positive memories you have of your loved ones who have passed.

Celebrate who they were, while allowing yourself time to grieve their unique presence. Don't let anyone dictate "how" or "how long" you grieve. Take all the time you need to mourn their passing. God knows and understands how you feel.

Remember your loved one for the beautiful and unique person they were. Hold on to that for your strength and comfort.

Allow warm memories to comfort you.

I walked into the kitchen and placed the grocery bags on the table. I noticed the "message waiting" light blinking on the answering machine and pressed the button to hear the message.

It was my mom's voice telling me the awful news of my friend's death. Lorna had been my best friend in high school and college. She'd been in a coma for weeks in the hospital—and now she'd passed away. The news was a total shock to me because when I visited her in the hospital, she opened her eyes as I sang to her.

When I think about Lorna's passing, I feel a piercing pain of sadness in my heart. It's okay to grieve and to cry when someone passes. It helps the healing process when you let it out and express your pain.

Lorna and I had a lot of good memories. She took me with her to apply for various colleges and we attended together. She took me to get my driver's license in her car. We started our own singing group and performed at local churches. There are so many happy memories that I choose to focus on when I feel the pain of her no longer being here.

Happy memories can ease the pain of a loved one who has passed. You are blessed that you were given the opportunity to have that person in your life. If your loved one was an unborn child, remember how you felt when you carried them in your belly. I'm sure you felt love for the wonderful miracle God placed inside you.

Squeeze out every happy memory you can and allow the memories to ease the sadness in your heart. You will never forget your loved one, and it will always hurt that they are no longer here, but hold on to the good memories and don't let them go.

Treasure the sweet memories of your loved one in your heart forever.

There are people who love you and care about you.

Most of the time, people don't know what to say to someone who is grieving. Even if you have lost a loved one, you will still never completely understand how someone else feels.

Everyone handles grief differently, and you can never know how someone feels inside when a loved one dies. One thing I have seen over and over though, is the love and compassion people show when someone is grieving. People come from all over to comfort a grieving family.

You may not see it right now, but there are people who love you and care about what you are going through. If you take a few minutes to look around, you will be able to sense the love and compassion from others as you grieve.

People would love to help you in any way they can, but often, they have no idea what to do. That's why you'll hear people say, "Let me know what I can do to help." They want to help, but they also realize they will never be able to ease your pain.

There are people in your life who are sincerely praying for your strength and comfort. Most people genuinely want you to feel loved and comforted.

Give yourself the space you need to cry and grieve—whenever you want to. Open your heart and receive the love that others offer when you are grieving. And when you feel like it, allow your loved ones to grieve with you. Remember, that they are hurting too.

When you cry, know that you aren't crying alone. Your friends and family love you and they care. They don't want you to give up on life. Take all the time you need to grieve, but don't let mourning take over your personality or stop you from living.

Let people in your heart and space to share the load with you. Others are grieving too and there is strength when we grieve together.

God knows your sorrow.

No one will ever really understand how you feel when a loved one dies. Even if they've experienced grief, they will never know exactly what is in your heart.

But God knows. God knows your sorrows. He is familiar with your grief.

God knows what it feels like to mourn someone you love. He understands the pain of saying goodbye to someone you will never see again.

The truth is, God knows your beginning and your end. He knows all about you. He holds the big picture of your life.

He knows when you will experience trials—job loss, divorce, sickness, and even the death of a loved one. He knows what you are going through and how you feel.

The amazing thing is that what we think about death is not what God thinks. We see what is in front of us. God looks on the inside. We see sickness and pain. God sees health and wholeness. We see the death of a loved one whom we will never see again. God sees eternal life.

We may never understand the big picture of our lives, but God does. He has already prepared everything we need. He provided a comforter for us in the form of the Holy Spirit. He is there to put His arms of comfort around us when we are overwhelmed with pain.

When your heart is piercing with grief, the Holy Spirit is there to comfort you. He will replace your suffering and despair with hope and renewal.

God knows how to bring beauty and meaning out of pain and devastation—just as He did through the death and resurrection of His Son, Jesus.

Have faith that everything will be alright. Allow the Holy Spirit to comfort you in your moments of distress.

God is with you. He knows your sorrow, and He cares about you. You will make it through this.

Personal Reflection

How will I make sure I take my own time grieving?

Prayer for When You are Mourning

Heavenly Father, thank You for blessing me with the time I did have
with my dear loved one.
I pray that You will give me strength to go on without them.
I pray for peace that passes all understanding.
I ask that You put Your loving arms around me, comfort me, and give me strength.
I pray that You will replace my mourning and heaviness
with a spirit of praise and thankfulness.
Help me to go forth in the freedom of Your peace to enjoy the rest of my life with
the family and friends who are still here.
In the name of Jesus I pray, Amen.

Bible Verse for When You are Mourning

Blessed are those who mourn, for they will be comforted.
Matthew 5:4

CHAPTER 12

When Life Seems Hopeless

You are stronger than you think.

David was a man in the bible who had so many unpredictable life experiences. At one point, his town was burned down and his family was taken captive by the enemy. David became deeply distressed, but he found strength in God and encouraged himself.

The Bible doesn't say how David encouraged himself, but because he was a musician, I wonder if he did so by playing his harp. You don't need a special talent to encourage yourself when you're feeling down. You already have the strength you need inside you, especially when you have God in your life.

You can lift your spirit and find encouragement from within. Sometimes, you might not have anyone you can talk to. Maybe you're that person who's always encouraging others, but you don't have anyone to encourage you when you're down.

When you're feeling down, try these ideas to encourage yourself when there is no one else to talk to:

- Speak to yourself with the same words of encouragement you would give someone else.

- Pray, sing, play music, or do something else that personally uplifts you.

- Buy yourself flowers or a thoughtful gift.

- Take yourself on a date.

- Go for a walk to clear your mind.

Don't let life keep you down. Lift your head up and encourage yourself.

There is a future for you.

We don't know what the future holds, but God does. God has a future for you. He created you for a reason and that reason is something only you can fulfill in this world. There is someone waiting for the gifts and talents you have to share.

Your future is bright because you are still here.

Feelings of depression can sometimes haunt you. Sadness and heaviness will come from nowhere. Depression will make you feel like life is hopeless, that your life does not matter, and that you are not loved. But, you *are* loved, your life *does* matter, and life is *not* hopeless.

There are still dreams within you to be fulfilled. You can still do the things you want to do. As long as you are alive and breathing, you can accomplish great things.

No one can be you but you. The world needs you and everything you have to offer. Be proud of who you are. Embrace your true self—good and bad. Every part of you makes up who you are and should be appreciated and respected. Everything God made is good, and He made you.

Hang in there, and don't let depression keep you down. When sadness hits, wait until it passes, and then go and do what you were born to do. Don't do anything drastic when you are feeling down. Pray, sing, or do something that personally uplifts you until the heaviness leaves.

Don't let sadness block your progress. Press forward and take the steps needed to accomplish your goals.

You have so many reasons to live and those reasons belong to you and no one else.

Hold on, change is coming.

Sometimes, life gets dark, and the pain seems too hard to bear. But if you hang on, things will get better.

When you're right in the middle of a trial, it can seem like there's no way out. You can't see any way out or how things will unfold. It seems like there is no hope and no use going on. But things always work out.

Regardless of what it looks like, things will get better.

Have you ever had pain in one part of your body and you think, *Man, this is the worst pain. If it were another part of my body, it wouldn't hurt as bad.* Then, when you feel pain in another part of your body, that pain feels like the worst pain ever.

When you're going through a trial, life seems hopeless at that moment, but the situation won't last forever. The depression and sadness you feel won't last forever. Be still and remain calm until it passes. It will pass.

Focus on how good life will be when the hopelessness passes. Think about the things that keep you going in life. You may not know it now, but there are great things in store for you. Wonderful surprises will come your way.

There will always be good days and bad days, but grab the good days and enjoy them. Don't let bad days get the best of you. You feel bad now, but you will feel better after a while.

Nothing in life ever stays the same and that includes bad times. Storm clouds eventually go away, and then the sun comes out. Hold on until you see the sunshine.

Stand strong, lift your head up, and hold on until your change comes.

You are the only one who can fulfill your destiny in this world. Don't give up. Hold on.

God is bigger and stronger than any problem.

There is so much noise in the world that it's easy to get distracted and pulled away from the things that really matter.

No matter what's going on in the world, remember that God is bigger and stronger than anything. Stay focused on the great things that have happened in your life. Keep good memories in front of your mind.

Count your blessings and the wonderful things that God has done for you—whether big or small.

When bad news makes you sad and filled with despair, encourage yourself by remembering that God loves you so much and wants to bless you with more than you can handle. He's blessed you before, and He can do it again.

God is omnipotent, which means He's all-powerful and unstoppable. He's able to give you the strength needed to move forward when you ask Him. He's omniscient, which means He is all-knowing and sees everything. He's able to work out any problem you will face. When darkness tries to pull you down, pull back and stand firm.

I fully believe in God and approach Him as my Heavenly Father. I believe He's the creator of the universe and the One who gives us breath each day. Keep walking in the light and strength of your Heavenly Father. Put your hand in God's hand to let Him lead the way.

When sickness gets you down, pray and pull yourself out of the muddy waters. Encourage yourself to move. Think about how God healed you before and be thankful for His healing power.

When life tries to get you down, get up, go outside, and lift your head up to the sky. Look at the vastness of the world that God created. God is all-powerful, and His strength lives inside you. He has plans for you.

Be grateful for your life and focus on the things that are going well.

Your life is meant to be celebrated.

When you take the time to think about it, you'll find so many things in your life to be thankful for. You can make your life great by celebrating one day at a time.

Instead of worrying about what could possibly happen months and years from now, focus on the good things in your life today. Anything can happen at any given time. Why not celebrate the good things that have happened already.

What is one thing you can celebrate today?

Each day gives you the opportunity to appreciate something in your life. Being able to live and breathe is a blessing that we should enjoy as much as we can.

Being able to spend time with family and friends is meaningful and should be celebrated. Family and friends provide the connections we need to thrive.

Every day, there is something to celebrate. Look at the magnificent things of nature that God created. There's so much beauty in the world to celebrate—the scenic sunrise that slowly rises each morning, the countless stars that twinkle in the night surrounding the bright moon, and the chirping birds that can sound like music when you listen closely.

Every new breath you take is another chance to celebrate life.

Regardless of what is going on in your life, don't forget to celebrate the good things. Make a list of the good things in your life—big and small—and be grateful for those. Revisit your list often to keep your blessings at the forefront of your mind and heart.

Every chance you get, celebrate the life you live.

Joyfulness is a choice.

Can you really choose to be happy and actually feel happy when things are going wrong in your life?

I used to wonder about this. Then, when I experienced situations that made me sad, I realized I could choose happiness. Even better, I could choose joy.

Choosing joy means you choose to smile and give yourself the freedom to be happy despite any touch situation you might face.

Just because you are going through something doesn't mean you have to allow it to stop you in your tracks from enjoying life.

When something happens in your life that catches you off guard, step back and tell yourself to be joyful anyway. Make the decision not to let anything get you down.

Practice positive self-talk and encourage yourself to move forward. Tell yourself you can make it. Tell yourself there is nothing that God cannot handle.

Pray and hope for the best in spite of what the situation looks like. Trust God to work everything out for you—because He will work it out.

Put your hand in God's hand to let Him lead you out of the situation and to the other side. He knows exactly how the situation will end, and He will pull you though it victoriously.

God will lead you like a father leads and takes care of his child.

Yes, it is tough right now. Yes, you are hurting, confused, knocked off your feet, but you're already victorious because God is fighting the battle for you.

Don't let the problem get you down. Keep moving forward to do the things you need to do to enjoy life. Pray about the situation, and then place it in God's hands. He can and will handle it.

Shake off the sadness. Choose joy.

Personal Reflection

What are my reasons for living when I feel like giving up?

Prayer for When Life Seems Hopeless

Heavenly Father, when I have no hope, You are my hope.
You are my reason for living.
You are the lifter of my soul. You are my joy and my strength.
There is nothing and no one greater than You.
You are my everything, and I put my trust in You to make everything alright.
In You, I do have hope because You have everything I need. I don't have to worry because You will take good care of me.
I don't have to despair because You provide everything I need.
You know the struggle and the pain I feel right now.
Please give me the strength I need to keep moving. Help me to carry on.
Amen.

Bible Verse for When Life Seems Hopeless

Then Jesus said, "Come to me, all of you who are weary and carry heavy burdens, and I will give you rest."
Matthew 11:28

Chapter 13
When You Are Lonely

Create love connections.

Loneliness is not so much about not having someone to love, it's more about not having connections. Establishing meaningful connections and nurturing relationships with family and friends can ease the frequent waves of loneliness in your life.

Consider these questions and actions to create meaningful love connections:

Who are the people in your life who truly know and understand you?
People who know you and are evolving with you understand you. They will be there for you as you walk through your life journey. Having people in your life whom you can be your authentic self around makes life so much easier.

Who are the people in your life who show up for you?
Having people you can call on in times of need is essential—these are the people you can trust to help without judgment or expecting a payback later. True connection is hard to find with anyone. Try your best to hold on to the special friendships in your life and cherish them.

Spend as much time as you can with family and friends. Those moments are meaningful and provide the connections you need to thrive.

Meeting new people can be fun. There is so much you can learn about other cultures when you meet people from various backgrounds. Look online or in your community for meet-up groups such as sports leagues, adventure clubs, travel groups, hiking teams, book clubs, or networking groups to find connections.

Be the person others would love to connect with. Reach out and show kindness to others and you will get the connections you desire. When you create love connections, you might find you're not as lonely as you thought you were.

Jesus loves you like no one else can.

There is no love that compares to the love of someone willing to give their life for another.

When Jesus gave His life for us on the cross, He was showing how much He passionately love us. The word passion comes from the Latin word passio, which comes from patior, meaning "to suffer". Suffer means to fear or endure pain. Jesus suffered extreme pain when He was nailed to the cross. I cannot think of a more passionate love than that. Jesus suffered torture for all of us. He even died for the men who nailed him to the cross that day.

Whether you are single and lonely or married and lonely, Jesus loves you passionately. He is not waiting for you to clean up your life, He loves you right where you are. He is not waiting for you to stop doing whatever you keep beating yourself up about. He loves you right now.

Even when you don't love yourself, Jesus loves you. All the things you criticize yourself for, He already knows about them and loves you anyway. He knows you better than you know yourself. He knew you would have weaknesses and struggles. That's why He accepted the torture and bruises to His body when He was crucified—to bear your struggles.

He knew you would have sickness and pain, that's why He endured the beatings that left ugly stripes on His back. Because of those stripes, you are already healed from any sickness you might encounter. Jesus knows and understands you when no one else does. He will never turn His back on you.

When you don't feel loved by anyone else, remember, Jesus loves you passionately and gave His life for you.

Jesus will never let you down. He will always be there for you. Receive His love today.

You are worth more than gold.

Rubies, diamonds, and pearls are all very beautiful gemstones. These stones are highly valuable, but guess what? You are worth more than any gemstone in this world. Gold is considered valuable because it can be exchanged for something else. But you could never be exchanged for someone else. There will never be anyone exactly like you.

You may be feeling alone and lonely right now, but it's not because you aren't attractive. You were created with love and beauty. Your very being can light up the world around you when you walk in the fullness of who you are.

You have so much to offer the world and those around you. You have so much potential to accomplish great things. There are wonderful gifts and talents inside you that will awaken when you intentionally use them. God gave you a unique personality. Never suppress who you truly are. The world needs to experience what you have to offer.

Honor your whole self (body, soul, and spirit) by doing the following:

- Protect your body from being used by those who have no idea of how much you are worth. Be kind to yourself physically through regular exercise that fits your style.

- Guard your soul and mind from worry and anything that would cheat you out of peace.

- Strengthen your spiritual core by staying in touch with God through prayer.

Love and respect the wonderful person God created you to be by daily nourishing your spirit, soul, and body. You are worth much more than gold and any precious gemstone. You are an invincible child of God.

Take care of your heart.

The offensive lineman's job in football is to block and to make sure the running back gets the ball down the field and makes a touchdown. When someone tries to approach the running back, the lineman blocks them or tackles them.

This is a great example of how to be an offensive lineman of your heart—guarding your heart to make sure you don't allow anything in that will weigh you down. Guarding your heart means blocking those things from your heart and mind that will keep you from thriving and moving forward.

Proverbs 4:23 (KJV) says, "Keep thy heart with all diligence for out of it are the issues of life." Our hopes and dreams come from our hearts. Our thoughts come from our heart. Our love for our family comes from our hearts. Our life purpose and relationship with God come from our heart.

It is so important that we guard our hearts from anything that could create obstacles to our life purpose.

What are your hopes and dreams? What is your vision for your life? What are you doing when you feel truly yourself? Protect those with your life. Don't let anything or anyone make you feel powerless.

Guard your heart from anything or anyone who tempts you to do things outside of what you know is right or what is truly you. Get in your lineman stance and be ready to block the dark times when they try to come. Get your game plan ready. Your game plan should include things that uplift and strengthen you personally.

Dark times will come, but the bright side is that you do have help. The Bible says in Philippians 4:13 (KJV), "I can do all things through Christ which strengthens me." Jesus Christ will strengthen you in your time of need.

Pray and ask God daily for strength to guard your heart from anything that would keep you from living a victorious life.

Personal Reflection

What can I do for positive social connection when I feel lonely?

Prayer for When You Are Lonely

Heavenly Father, I feel alone and lonely right now.
I have no one to love. I don't want to grow old alone.
I want someone to share my life with. I want to feel loved.
Please help me on this journey.
Fill my heart with more of You so that I am fulfilled daily.
Help me to stay focused on my purpose
and to not be drawn into compromising situations.
Help me to enjoy this phase of my life and
not wait for someone else to make me happy.
I know that even though I feel lonely sometimes,
I know that you are always with me.
Thank You for sending people into my life
to remind me of Your love for me.
I will cherish the love connections on my journey.
Thank you, God. Amen.

Bible Verse for When You Are Lonely

I am leaving you with a gift—peace of mind and heart.
And the peace I give is a gift the world cannot give.
So don't be troubled or afraid.
John 14:27

CHAPTER 14

When You Are Struggling with Being Single

Even though you are single, you are not alone.

Next to my college days, being a divorced single was one of the loneliest times of my life. There were moments when I was so lonely, it felt unbearable. I was desperate for someone to love and for someone to love me. Then, just in the nick of time, my life was filled with so many activities that I didn't have time to feel lonely.

I got involved in local church singles events and went out almost every weekend with activities like bowling, dinner, movies, and game night with a circle of safe friends.

God knows you need someone in your life. He knows you get lonely sometimes and just at the right time, He will send reminders that He is with you by sending positive people into your life.

You could meet a new acquaintance, reconnect with a good friend, or even bump into a former admirer. These "chance encounters" are reminders that God is with you and cares about the loneliness you feel. God knows you need "connection" and will send people your way when you need it most.

Learning to enjoy life as a fulfilled single person is critical before you move into marriage. When you learn how to enjoy your life as it is now, you will have a strong foundation for who you are when you move into marriage.

Be prayerful and hopeful. Talk to God about your desire for companionship. Be open to who He has for you and remove all reservations and unrealistic requirements.

You are not alone. Someone is with you who loves you, cares for you, and has a great future for you. Stay close to Him during this phase in your life and enjoy where you are now.

God is there to help you when you need it.

There was a man in the Bible who was disabled for 38 years. He lived in Jerusalem, near a pool called Bethesda. Disabled people would lie around the pool waiting for the water to stir. When it did, they would get into the pool, hoping to be healed.

Jesus was in Jerusalem for one of the Jewish festivals and saw a man lying near the pool. He learned that the man had been disabled for a long time. He asked the man if he wanted to get well.

The man replied, *"Sir, I have no one to help me into the pool when the water is stirred. While I am trying to get in, someone else goes ahead of me."*

Jesus said to him, *"Get up. Pick up your mat and walk."*

The man was immediately healed, picked up his mat, and walked.

This story reminds me that God is always there when we need Him. Maybe you have been waiting for years to meet that special someone. Maybe you have been waiting for someone to "help you get into the pool" or waiting for "the one."

If you ever feel lonely and need a friend, don't wait for someone to find you. God already knows where you are. God has everything you need. Talk to Him about how you feel.

When you don't feel loved, don't give up. God loves you and He cares about you. He can love you better than anyone else can, because He knows all about you.

Don't wait for man to comfort you because men will sometimes let you down. God is always loyal to bless you with exactly what you need for your life.

Just like the man at the pool of Bethesda received God's help and healing, you can too. Trust and depend on God for everything you need, and He will make a way for you.

Enjoy the journey.

Life is a journey. It starts when you are born, and it ends when you leave this earth. Wouldn't life be better if you enjoyed the journey?
Here are some ideas for enjoying the journey while you are single:

- Explore ways that you can help the people you were created to help. What groups of people are you drawn to help? Serving those who tug at your heart will give you a deep sense of fulfillment and will help you enjoy your life's journey.

- Try new things. Visit new places, try new food, start a new hobby, join a meet-up group such as a sports league, adventure club, travel group, hiking team, book club, or networking group.

- When you go out and do things you enjoy, be open to meeting someone new. This could lead to a relationship with someone who enjoys doing the same things you do.

Instead of waiting for marriage, enjoy this part of your journey. If your journey does lead to marriage, then you'll know who you are and what you enjoy doing when you shift into marriage.

When you live a full single life, you will be able to invite that special someone into a solid life you have built for yourself.

Look on the bright side of your independence and freedom. You have your own space to create what you want, the way you want. Focus on creating the perfect life for you. Enjoy the journey where you are, and make the best of life.

The grass is not always greener on the other side.

The grass always looks greener on the other side. Social media posts can make everything look perfect, but believe me, things are not always as they seem. People typically post the best of the best and rarely air their dirty laundry online, and that's okay. They shouldn't. But remember. Photos often present a more glamorous lifestyle than what the person really has.

Even celebrities look much better than they naturally look because of expensive beauty enhancements. They have to look a certain way in order to be successful in Hollywood.

Don't be swayed by the "false advertising" online. Be content with what you have, because what you have is good. What you have was meant for you.

Be grateful for your home and take care of it like it's the million-dollar mansion you see on television. Wherever you live is your home. Be grateful that you have somewhere to lay your head. Be proud that you have a place to call home.

You may not have a $80,000 vehicle, but whatever you have is yours. Wash it and drive it like it is your dream car. Whatever you drive gets you from point A to point B, and that means it's a good car.

Be proud of your children and don't compare them to other people's children. They are your children and God trusted you with their care. Celebrate your child's accomplishments like they just won the Nobel peace prize. Love them, nourish them, and build them up to live to their potential.

Be grateful for what you have, and you'll be the richest person on earth, because you'll have joy, peace, and contentment.

You are wonderful, all by yourself. You don't need anyone or anything to make you look good. You may not be where you want to be in life, but you are here, and there are great things in store for you.

Personal Reflection

What are some activities I can start doing to make sure I'm enjoying the journey of being single?

Prayer for When You Are Struggling with Being Single

Heavenly Father, as You know, I'm not content with my life right now. I'm not happy about being single. I desire companionship. I don't feel like doing a whole lot with my life right now.

I'm wondering if You're ever going to send me a mate.

I know You created me for a reason, and I ask that You reveal my purpose so I can live a fulfilling life whether I'm single or married.

Lord, please give me strength and peace of mind.

Help me to be content with my life. Please remove any feelings of doubt, discontentment, and unhappiness.

Fill my heart with gladness as I enjoy life one day at a time. Thank you, God. Amen

Bible Verse for When You Are Struggling with Being Single

Take delight in the Lord,
and he will give you your heart's desires.
Psalm 37:4

CHAPTER 15

When You Are Struggling with Marriage

Marriage is a roller coaster. Enjoy the ride.

I've heard people say that marriage is hard work. I prefer to say it like this: marriage is a roller coaster. There are times when you're at the top of the roller coaster tracks of marriage—high in the air and high on the joys of life.

Other times, you have some steep drops of trials and tribulations. Sometimes in marriage, you have sudden changes of direction, where you might have to change some major goals and plans. Then, you have the occasionally exciting loops of fun surprises.

There is also a coasting phase in marriage where you have done the "hard work" of communication, therapy, forgiving, and compromising and you are just coasting. This is a sweet phase, but make sure you're both comfortable there. You might be comfortable while your partner wants more excitement or vice versa.

Couples who have been married for over 30, 40, and 50 years are often asked what the key to a happy marriage is. Every couple has a different answer to that question because there is no "one size fits all" key to marriage. What works for someone else's marriage might not work for yours.

I believe to have a long-term marriage, you must be willing to stay on the roller coaster during every phase.

Every marriage will have ups and downs, but if you hang in there, you'll get to a point where you're coaxing and enjoying the ride. Continue to communicate, forgive, and even get counseling when needed. Don't give up when times get hard.

Remember that you and your spouse are a team. You're on the roller coaster together. Support each other through the ride. Don't let anything or anyone pull you apart while both of you do the work needed to stay together.

Every day is an opportunity to start fresh.

Whatever happened yesterday is over. This is a new day to start fresh. This is a new day to forgive and forget.

Sometimes, marital problems start happening because something is missing in the marriage. What's missing is usually connected to a lack of emotional or physical intimacy.

Lack of intimacy can cause coldness and disconnection in a marriage. It takes both people in the marriage to maintain a healthy level of intimacy.

Often, one person puts forth effort to maintain some level of emotional or physical intimacy, but the other person has "checked out." The "checking out" could be voluntary due to a loss of interest or it could be involuntary due to health issues or life trauma.

If you are doing all you can to maintain intimacy in your marriage and you still feel lost, empty, lonely, or rejected, don't give up.

Here are some things you can try to start fresh:

Remind yourself of the person you fell in love with. What attracted you to him or her?

Shape your thoughts around the feelings you had when you first met. Allow the excitement of those new beginnings to reenter your frame of mind.

Try something different to rekindle the spark.

Relive the magic of your first date—recreate that unforgettable evening. Get hands-on in the kitchen and cook a delicious meal together. Dive into something new—take a dance class or paint class. Surprise each other with sweet love notes hidden in unexpected places. Lighten their load by taking over their chores. Plan a dreamy picnic under the stars or a sunny afternoon escape, complete with all their favorite treats. Step into their world—what little (or big) gesture would sweep them off their feet? Be bold, be thoughtful, and watch your love story renew.

Instead of seeking outside attention, flirt with your spouse.

Reignite that spark by being playful, affectionate, and irresistibly charming. Send a steamy text out of the blue, whisper a compliment that makes them blush, or sweep them off their feet with an unexpected massage. Surprise them with their favorite treat… and follow it up with something even sweeter.

Keep the romance alive—flirt like you're still falling for each other!

When you're struggling in your marriage, shake up the routine—steal kisses, whisper compliments, and chase each other like you're falling in love all over again. Break the ordinary, stand stronger together, and fill your life with adventures, laughter, and passion.

Your love story is worth writing every single day.

Prayer changes things.

I know it sounds cliché, but prayer really does change things. There have been so many situations in my marriage where I sincerely prayed, and the situation changed.

I like to think of God as our Heavenly Father who is watching over us and taking care of us. And guess what? God is watching over and taking care of our spouse too. That means when you pray about your partner, God is looking at both of you to determine what's best for your marriage. He's not taking sides. He doesn't want either of you to suffer.

When your spouse has done something to hurt you, talk to God about it. Let Him know how much it hurt you. Pray that God will deliver your spouse from whatever causes them to do wrong and pray for yourself in the process. Take the time and space you need to heal from pain.

God already knows your mate and what makes them tick. He knows them better than you do. Trust that He will work on them and do what needs to be done. Don't try to work on them yourself. Trying to change your spouse will only lead to resentment on both sides. Pray for patience and mercy in your heart. Ask God to give you wisdom for the situation—and He will.

When you pray, God will do what any father would—He will handle the situation in a way that will correct whoever needs to be corrected and will reconcile the love that was lost. You'll be surprised at how the most tough situations in your marriage will work out when you pray about them.

Say a sincere prayer for yourself and your spouse. Be humble and willing to make any necessary changes—as long as they aren't harmful to you.

When you pray for your spouse, yourself, and your marriage, everything will work together for your good.

You are responsible for your actions and reactions.

Sometimes, anger can lead people to punch a wall, cuss someone out, throw things, scratch a car, and flatten somebody's tires. Regardless of what someone says or does to you, your reaction should never be as bad or worse than their actions.

It's normal to get angry, but you shouldn't let your emotions take complete control. When you allow anger to get the best of you, you may say or do things you'll regret later.

Regardless of the wrong people do to you, try your best not to add insult to injury. Don't make matters worse by reacting outrageously when someone mistreats you. The situation is already bad; a hostile reaction won't make it better. Try your best to communicate calmly with those involved to come to a peaceful resolution.

Sometimes, you may need to step away from the situation until everyone is calm. Then come together—possibly with a mediator or counselor—for peaceful resolution. A good counselor can be helpful in translating messages between married couples, especially when they have trouble expressing themselves.

The next time you feel yourself getting angry, take a deep breath, pause, and think about the consequences of what you will say or do. Try your best to control your emotions.

Put yourself in the other person's shoes and respond with the loving response you would want if you were the one who messed up.

Stay until the miracles happen.

I often wonder what kind of trials couples who have been married 30, 40, or even 50 years have experienced. I know they had to go through some tough spots to make it so far.

They made it through the fight. They forgave. They might not have forgotten but they didn't keep bringing it up. They moved on. They made it through mourning, financial hardship, and layoffs. They stayed and worked through things together until the miracles happened.

The miracles are those beautiful benefits and results that happen when you commit to each other. The miracle of finally getting to the point of forgiveness and trust after betrayal. The miracle of healing after the passing of a child. The miracle of restoration and renewal after emotional or physical infidelity. These are the miracles that can happen when you hang in there through the tough times.

A lot of people don't stay long enough to see the miracles happen. They give up too soon. Yes, marriage gets hard, and sometimes it seems like it won't last. You might feel like throwing in the towel sometimes and saying, "Forget it!" But if you hang in there, you will see miracles. You won't see the miracles if you quit. Miracles surpass all known human or natural powers. Only God can work miracles.

If you stay and work through the problems, you won't even recognize your marriage down the road because the miracles will transform it. When you feel like giving up, don't. Hold on. Lovingly communicate with each other about your issues. Get couples therapy when you need effective tools to navigate tough times.

One day, you will see the miracles in your marriage if you hang in there and work together.

Stay true to who you are.

When you marry, you become one with your partner. You share your home, finances, household responsibilities, and goals for the future, as you build your life together. Although you are united as one, God gave each of you unique gifts and talents. It's important to continue using those gifts and talents to fulfill your purpose in life.

It's also important to stay true to who you are, because your partner married you for you. Bringing your authentic self into the marriage is one of the greatest gifts you can give your spouse.

You are blessed with unique gifts to share with the world and help others in some capacity. If you stop being who you truly are, you may miss the connection you could make with the people you were designed to reach.

Your gifts and talents should not be hidden when you get married.

Continue to let your true personality show wherever you go. And while you work on things with your partner, be sure to take care of yourself—mentally and emotionally.

Try not to stress yourself out with worry. Do things you enjoy even if you have to do them alone. Engaging in activities you enjoy will keep your mind occupied and prevent you from worrying. This will help maintain your mental health.

On days when your spouse seems emotionally distant or has "checked out," what can you do to care for your own mental and emotional health?

It's not uncommon for opposite personalities to attract each other. But try not to change your personality to mirror your spouse's, and don't try to mold your spouse into someone they're not. You'll be stronger together when you both live your authentic self.

Give each other space to be yourselves, and watch your marriage grow stronger as you both develop individually and grow together.

Personal Reflection

What are some things I can do to maintain my personal well-being while my marriage is struggling?

Prayer for When You are Struggling With Marriage

Heavenly Father, help me to be a good spouse
while I also nourish the personality You gave me.
Marriage is hard right now, but I thank You for this time because it makes me pray more. Lord, I ask You to teach me how to be more loving. Regardless of who is at fault, I pray that You will work on me.
Show me how to love my spouse, and show my spouse how to love me. Give us the wisdom we need to make this marriage work. Teach both of us Your way. Show us how to walk better together as one.
Thank You, God. Amen.

Bible Verse for When You are Struggling With Marriage

Love is patient and kind. Love is not jealous or boastful or proud or rude.
It does not demand its own way.
It is not irritable, and it keeps no record of being wronged.
It does not rejoice about injustice but rejoices whenever the truth wins out.
Love never gives up, never loses faith, is always hopeful,
and endures through every circumstance.
1 Corinthians 13:4-7

CHAPTER 16

When You Have Been Hurt

You are a victor, not a victim.

Yes, you have been hurt, but you are strong. Although you are a victim in this situation, do not allow this setback to cause you to act like a victim. Get up, wash away the dirt, and keep moving. You can—and you will—make it through this.

Don't allow your pain to control your emotions or dictate how you act and react. Walk and talk like the victorious person you are.

Instead of allowing the betrayal to destroy you, use it to show how strong you are. You are more than a conqueror. You are a winner.

Unfortunately, there are people in this world who rob, steal, and scam others. The betrayal of someone close seems to hurt more than that of a stranger, because we don't expect it. When someone hurts you, don't stay down in the dumps. Make the decision that you're not going to let it keep you down.

Here are some things you could do when you're hurting:

- **Instead of feeling sorry for yourself, take time to pray about your situation.** Ask God to give you the strength to make it through. Then lift your head up and move forward in victory.

- **Conquer the painful feelings of whatever you're going through.** Don't sit around sulking. Be a winner by telling yourself you can make it.

- **Speak faith to yourself.** Encourage yourself. Pump yourself up and keep moving forward in spite of the pain.

A victorious person is someone who defeats the enemy's attack. Attacks will come, but you will win! Don't give up. Keep the faith. Push through the pain, and you'll come out victorious on the other side.

You can make it through this.

It's tough right now, but you can make it. You've had hard times before, and you made it through. God brought you through hard times before. He will do it again.

I know you don't know how this will turn out. You're probably wondering how you'll be able to make it through, but you will.

Right now, you feel weak and confused. You don't know where to turn. You don't have anyone you can tell your troubles to. Everyone seems preoccupied with their own problems. That's okay—you'll be fine.

If you're unable to talk to someone about what you're going through, grab a journal and write your feelings out. You might be surprised at how much better you feel when you put your thoughts on paper. Write honestly, and if you're concerned someone might find what you wrote, destroy the paper afterwards.

You feel like you're all alone, but you're not. God is with you. He is right there. Just put your hand in His. You don't know how things will turn out, but God does.

Put your hand in God's hand and let Him lead the way. No matter how low you feel, God can reach down and pull you out of your deepest and darkest sadness.

Take a deep breath, say a prayer, and trust that God will work everything out. He's moving behind the scenes of your life. You only see what's happening around you. God knows the background, the hidden story, and the ultimate plot.

When this is all over, you'll be the victor of the battle, the conqueror of the enemy, the winner of the fight.

Don't trust what you see—trust God's promise to make everything all right for you.

Have faith. You can—and you will—make it through.

Personal Reflection

What will I do to maintain a victor's mentality while I am healing from being hurt?

Prayer for When You Have Been Hurt

Lord, I am in so much pain now from what is happening.
Help me make it through.
I cannot see my way, but I know You see everything.
Give me patience, love, strength, and comfort as I go through this battle.
Help me to be victorious.
I am weak right now, please be my strength.
Thank You, God, Amen.

Bible Verse for When You Have Been Hurt

> He heals the brokenhearted
> and bandages their wounds.
> Psalm 147:

CHAPTER 17

When You Are Sick

Feed your atmosphere with hope.

I walked into the hospital room to visit a friend who was sick with cancer. As she lay there in bed, I barely recognized her—the horrible sickness had taken over her body. But as soon as she spoke, I immediately felt the loving and joyful spirit that I was familiar with.

As I sat there talking to her, there were other people in the room who were saying all kinds of negative things. There was constant complaining and words filling the air with worry and despair. I couldn't bear it—I kindly asked the nurse if we could have some quiet time alone. Once the room cleared, the atmosphere lifted to a positive one.

When you're sick and bed-ridden, it's critical to create an atmosphere of hope wherever you are. Hope can lighten the heaviness that often comes from worrying about your situation.

When you're sick and bed-ridden, so many negative thoughts can enter your mind and cause you to fear what lies ahead. When you intentionally turn your focus to positive thoughts and prayers, it will strengthen your faith that everything will be alright.

When your body is in pain, say a prayer and force yourself to sing a song or play your favorite music. Music has the power to heal, especially when the lyrics are positive and uplifting. The right kind of music will make a difference in how you feel and will create a spirit of healing in the room.

Create an atmosphere of hope by remembering times you have overcome sickness before. Think about the things you have to be grateful for. Try your best to maintain a positive outlook for your future.

If you're able, spend some time outdoors to get a little sunlight.

Focus on the big picture of life, realizing that what you are experiencing is only temporary.

Praising God in advance for your healing can ease the pain.

What if we could be joyful during sickness? What if we could smile and dance even while we're confused and don't know what's going on in our bodies?

When we're waiting for a medical diagnosis, we have all kinds of thoughts of what could possibly go wrong. Then, when the situation is over, we find out it wasn't as bad as we feared. We realize the prognosis wasn't what the internet search results said it might be.

If we pray and keep our hopes up through sickness, our days could be brighter.

If we sing and look up while we're hurting, we could accomplish more, because we wouldn't be sitting idle thinking doom and gloomy thoughts. I remember times when I was so sick, I could hardly think straight. I would turn on my gospel music playlist, and the music would immediately lift my spirits and calm my mind.

Have you ever received a request from someone, and they thanked you in advance for considering it? It's a thoughtful gesture to thank someone in advance. It lets the person know you appreciate any effort or thought they will give towards their request.

The next time you are hit with sickness, make the decision to thank God in advance for your healing. God already knows He is going to work everything together for your good, so why not thank Him in advance for what He is going to do?

God's got you. He is a healer and deliverer. All power is in His hands.

Trust God. He's working everything out, so praise Him now, in advance for your healing.

Encourage yourself.

Words have power. They can destroy and they can create. Sometimes a single word can change everything.

There have been times when I was lying in bed, sick and in pain, and I turned on my favorite music—and immediately started feeling better. There's something about creating an atmosphere of hope through words or music that helps ease emotional pain and worry when you're sick.

I've also found that speaking words of faith and trusting in God helps you feel better. When you express your trust in God's ability to heal, the load will feel lighter because you're giving it over to someone you know can handle it better than you can.

When you pray for healing, your perspective of your illness changes. You know you've put it in God's hands, and it's no longer your burden to bear.

When you say negative things about your situation, it'll make you feel worse. For some reason, grumbling about a problem seems to give legs to the issue and make it bigger.

When you are experiencing sickness, use words that build yourself and others. Be your own best supporter, and be the voice for those around you to help build their faith. The more people you have rooting for you, the stronger the synergy and healing atmosphere will be in the room.

Speaking God's Word for your healing adds power to your circumstance. Quoting a Bible verse like "I can do all things through Christ who strengthens me" can give you the courage and power to keep moving when you feel like giving up.

If you receive a horrible diagnosis, pray and express your trust in God while you receive the treatment you need. This will give you peace while you wait for your healing.

If there are times when you cannot find the right words to say, just say, "It's all good" or be silent. Sometimes silence will calm the noisy thoughts in your head while God is working things out for you.

Regardless of what you go through, speak words of hope. Everything will be alright in the end.

You will eventually see your way.

As I was driving up the steep highway, rain poured down so hard I could barely see the lane markings clearly. I was terrified. I passed a sign showing the grade of the highway incline, and it only heightened my fear—it confirmed just how steep the road really was.

I looked for somewhere to pull over but because of the heavy rain, the huge 18-wheelers speeding by, and the highway slope, there was nowhere for me to stop. I finally made it through the storm and saw the sunshine at the end of the highway.

I learned a valuable metaphor for life that day—just push through the storm and you will eventually see your way.

How many times have you been in a desperate situation, and you didn't know how you would get out of it? You didn't see any way out. Thinking back on those times, you probably feel blessed.

When you're in the middle of a life-threatening diagnosis, it's scary. You don't know how it will end or how you'll make it out, but God always brings you out.

When sickness and pain are robbing you of all joy and you can't see your way, just keep pushing through. Don't give up on life. God is right there with you. He's with you in the middle of the storm.

God will hold your hand while you go through the rain, the medical tests, the treatment, and will be with you, helping you make it to the other side.

You have had hard times before, and you made it through. Keep holding on to your faith. You can and you will make it through this.

The clear skies and the sunshine are there waiting for you. Push through the rain until you see the sunshine.

Keep your hand in God's hands, and He will see you through.

Personal Reflection

What positive words will I say to myself and others while I am in the process of healing?

Prayer for When You are Sick

Heavenly Father, I ask for Your healing touch.
Please remove the pain and suffering I am feeling.
I ask You to restore my health.
I believe in Your power and mercy, and I know You are able to work miracles.
Give me strength and patience as I recover from this illness.
I give my whole body to You, Lord, and I trust in Your perfect will. I praise and glorify Your name on this journey.
In the powerful name of Jesus I pray. Amen.

Bible Verse for When You are Sick

He personally carried our sins
in his body on the cross
so that we can be dead to sin
and live for what is right.
By his wounds you are healed.
1 Peter 2:24

CHAPTER 18

When You are Discontent

God opens and closes doors based on what is best for you.

I received the phone call I had been waiting for: "April, we would like you to come in to interview for the position." My heart jumped with excitement. This was a position I really wanted.

Within weeks, I completed all the interviews and then waited for the job offer. It never came. This happened several times over the course of my career—one door would open for a great opportunity and when I didn't get the job, another door would open for something better.

It's normal to be discouraged when you don't receive a job offer you want and sometimes need. There's so much effort that goes into writing a resume and preparing for an interview, and when you don't get the job offer, it is disappointing.

The bright side of not receiving the job offer is that God always knows what's best for you. He knows where you should be. He will open doors for you that should be open and will close doors that should be closed in your life.

Your career path might not always start where you envision, but every opportunity is a chance to grow. No experience is wasted—each role equips you with valuable skills, resilience, and insight that will propel you forward. There are lessons for you to learn until something better comes along.

God will close doors in places that He knows would not be good for you. They might look attractive because of the pay, location, or other reasons, but God closes those doors when there is something about the job that would not fit into His plans for your life. Stay focused, keep learning, and trust that every step you take is bringing you closer to your dreams.

Moving through life should happen at your own pace.

For years, I commuted almost two hours each way to work on a busy interstate in Texas where there were accidents every single day.

My driving strategy was to stay in one lane for as much of the commute as possible. Since I usually drive the speed limit, I would remain in the slow lane to allow other drivers to pass as needed.

At times, other drivers would pull up quickly behind me, trying to coerce me into speeding up. But I would never do that because I was in the slow lane. It was their responsibility to switch to the fast lane if they wanted to go faster.

This type of behavior reminds me of the peer pressure you might sometimes feel when you see other people advancing in their career. You might ask yourself, *Why am I still where I am and other people have better jobs?*

If you allow the fast drivers to pressure you into moving faster than you normally would, it could cause problems because you're not moving at your natural pace.

You know how much you can handle on your plate. You know when you are at your best. Move at your own pace.

Move at a speed that is comfortable and suitable for you. The only expectations you should strive to meet are your own. Use your own measuring stick to determine your progress.

What is your vision for yourself?

Compare yourself to your own vision and don't rush to get there. Be inspired by the vision of how you see yourself in the future.

Take baby steps and move at your own natural pace to accomplish your goals.

Disappointment is a good thing.

It's normal to feel disappointment. Go ahead and embrace it. Disappointment means you have goals and desires. It also means you're living life and still have opportunities.

Maybe disappointment has raised his ugly head in your life when the marriage didn't happen when you wanted. There are no children yet. You still don't have the salary you wanted at this age.

It's okay to be disappointed because it will give you the drive to keep hoping. If there is more you want to accomplish, accept where you are right now but stay alert to learn what you need to do to grow.

Everyone moves at their own pace in life. It takes some people three years to get a college degree and others over ten years. It doesn't matter how long it takes. What matters is that you're on a journey to get there, and you'll eventually get there. Enjoy the journey until you get there.

Live your life being excited and hopeful that you're moving from point A to point B. So what if it takes you longer than you planned to get to point B. Enjoy yourself on your way there. If it helps you feel better, try making a checklist of baby steps it will take you to get from Point A to Point B. Celebrate each time you complete a baby step, because each step moves you closer to your goal.

Don't, under any circumstances, compare yourself to other people's progress. Their journey is not yours. You have your own journey, your own challenges, and your own wins.

Let disappointment push you to complete your baby steps and eventually complete your goals.

You will reach your goals one day and you will be able to celebrate all the hard work you're doing now to get there.

Small beginnings lead to huge wins.

After I graduated from college, I had a hard time finding a job. I had several interviews, but was told I didn't have enough work experience. I ended up settling for a temporary file clerk position at a state agency. I was disappointed that I couldn't attain a position that matched the bachelor's degree I earned.

While I worked in that position, the regional director approached me one day and called me into her office. We discussed my future and opportunities with the agency. Shortly after our conversation, I was promoted to a permanent position that led to a management-level role.

My career advancement didn't stop there. I was approached by a manager of another department in the agency, asking me to replace her because she was moving to another position. I worked in that role for years and gained skills that I used to move into corporate America. At one point in my career, I advanced to an Assistant Vice-President position at a Fortune 500 bank. Who knew a state file clerk position would lead to better jobs for me, a wonderful career I loved, and eventually a lifetime pension that would contribute to my early retirement?

Do not despise your humble beginnings. Humble beginnings could lead to great finishes. You may have to start at the bottom and work your way up to the top. You may have to accept positions you don't want at times just to get your foot in the door to reach your goals. Learn all you can in the position you are in. Work like you are the CEO of the company, and let it reflect in your behavior and work ethics. Your hard work could lead to promotions and future opportunities.

Appreciate the small jobs that you think are insignificant. This job is only the beginning of greater things you will achieve.

This is all part of your growth on your journey.

Personal Reflection

What are my goals for the next 5, 10, and 15 years? What baby steps can I take now to reach my goals?

Prayer for When You are Discontent

Heavenly Father, I pray that You will open doors that should be opened in my life and close doors that should be closed. I pray that my plans will ultimately align with Your plans for my life.

Help me to keep my eyes and ears open to be able to see how You are guiding me.

I pray for favor in job interviews for the jobs You have for me.

Give me the patience to do every job to the best of my ability, as if I am working for You.

Use the struggles and challenges that I encounter at work to build muscles and knowledge for the promotions I will receive later.

When I try to do things that aren't on the path You have for me, please block my way.

Change my plans when I move in a direction that is not in Your will.

Lord, I ask that You bless me to prosper financially even as I prosper spiritually.

Help me to enjoy my career journey in whatever job I do. Amen.

Bible Verse for When You are Discontent

If you are faithful in little things,
you will be faithful in large ones.
But if you are dishonest in little things,
you won't be honest with greater responsibilities.
Luke 16:10

Chapter 19

When You Are Having Trouble at Work

Change the atmosphere. Do not let the atmosphere change you.

I stepped into the hotel conference room and heard the grumbling and complaining about the weather, the hotel food, and other inconveniences.

As everyone voiced their opinions, they looked at me and waited for me to share my grievances. I felt the pressure to complain, but instead of giving in, I decided to try and change the atmosphere. I talked about the good food we had enjoyed, shared tips for better sleep on the road, and brought up highlights from the day's agenda. Before long, the energy in the room shifted—laughter replaced complaints, and smiles overtook frowns.

This is a simple example, but it shows how you can change a negative environment with positive conversation. There will always be some type of conflict at work.

Take these steps to change the atmosphere of negative situations:

1. Assess the situation to see where the negativity started.

2. Lead by example. Stay calm, respectful, and kind.

3. Encourage mutual support if you see personal conflicts.

4. Maintain your energy. Don't get caught up in the negativity.

5. In extreme cases, it might be necessary for you to remove yourself from the environment.

By taking these steps, you can gradually shift a negative atmosphere to a positive space for yourself wherever you are. You could give hope to someone in the group by looking on the bright side.

Look for meaningful moments throughout your day.

Finding meaningful moments throughout your day can help you through some of the toughest times. Whether you're working in the office or remote, there are always opportunities to find meaningful moments throughout your day.

There is always something new to be thankful for every day. Every breath you take is new. Every sun or cloud you see every day is new. Each new day gives you a chance to say something new to a relative or friend.

Try these ideas to find meaningful moments in your day:

- Take a few moments to focus on the present. What do you see, hear, smell, or feel that you can be thankful for?

- Notice what is going well in your day that you can be grateful for. It could be something as simple as a good cup of coffee or tea.

- Slow down and fully engage with the world and the people around you. You might be surprised with a pleasant experience.

- If you are able to, step outside and notice the sound of birds and the blue sky. Sometimes just a little sunlight will brighten your day.

By intentionally looking for meaningful moments, you can create a more fulfilling day at work. The moments don't have to be huge—most of the time they're found in the small everyday details that we overlook.

Always giving your best will keep you on track.

Sometimes work can be difficult, especially when you are working with difficult people or a difficult manager. To help your workday run smoother, start by shifting your mindset. Hold yourself accountable to a personal set of values, beliefs, and goals regarding work. Remind yourself of the personal financial benefits you will gain by working and being responsible.

Own your work and take pride in what you do. If you were the owner of the company, you would want your employees to be committed.

When you're committed to the work you do, this will give you a sense of accomplishment. You will have pride in knowing you're doing your best.

If you don't feel appreciated, empower yourself by taking personal action to do what you agreed to do. Decide on the steps you'll take to do your job successfully. Ask for assistance if you need it to avoid feeling overwhelmed.

If there're some things that are preventing you from working productively or safely, let management know. Keep following up until the issues are resolved.

Do a personal evaluation and ask yourself, "Is there something I need to learn about myself in this situation?" Sometimes there's a quality that needs to be strengthened. Pay close attention to your attitude and where you need to improve.

When you're at work, give your full attention to your job. When you're involved in too many personal activities during work hours, your job will seem like an annoyance to you. There's a time for work and a time for play.

Celebrate your success on the job. As you work with integrity and responsibility, you'll be rewarded in one way or another. When you sow seeds of integrity through your job, God will reward you with benefits you might not see now, but you will definitely see later.

It's best to wish the best for your enemies.

Be one of the loving and kind people that others need to see in the world. Instead of returning evil for evil, show gentleness and thoughtfulness.

Be sincere in hoping that those who have wronged you find peace and happiness. Don't harbor resentment for them. Rise above negativity and conflict and focus on inner peace and emotional freedom.

You would only be hurting yourself if you tried to avenge your enemies. Everything you do to others will come back to you in one way or another.

The same goes for showing kindness.

You might meet people in your life who dislike you for no reason whatsoever. Maybe you remind them of someone unpleasant—a teacher, former manager or co-worker, sister, or brother. Don't let their actions affect how you treat them. Instead of treating them the way they treat you, make the decision in your heart to hope for the best for their life.

It's a lot easier to show love to those who have intentionally harmed you than it is to be vengeful. It takes time and effort to think about how to get back at someone. You could use that time for something more productive like moving forward in your life. Vengeance traps you into a dark ugly place that will be hard to get out of, and you'll have a hard time moving forward.

Sometimes, people are angry or mean because of horrible things going on in their life. They take their problems out on others. The way they treat you might have nothing to do with you. Take the posture of compassion and kindness towards them. Maybe this will soften their heart.

Wishing the best for your enemies is not about condoning their actions. It's about choosing a path of peace for you and those around you. Your gentleness could be contagious and encourage your enemies to do the same.

Personal Reflection

What is the bright side of where I am right now in my career?

Prayer for When You Are Having Trouble at Work

Lord, thank You for blessing me with this job.
Thank You for the opportunity to learn new skills.
Please give me the strength and wisdom to work to the best of my ability.
Help me to show love and kindness to everyone on the job.
I pray for promotions, advancement, and better jobs according to Your plan for my life. Amen.

Bible Verse For When You are Having Trouble at Work

Work willingly at whatever you do, as though you were working for the Lord rather than for people.
Colossians 3:23

CHAPTER 20

When You Are Dealing with Difficult People

Looking for the best in everyone can reveal the best to you.

God created everyone on this earth, regardless of how difficult some people might be. **Try this approach the next time you face difficult people:**

- **Try to find their positive qualities.** Put away all the prejudgments you have about them and look for their positive qualities. Even if you only find one positive—focus on that. They might just improve their behavior when they see your expectations.

- **Put yourself in their shoes and ask, "How would I want to be treated if I acted this way?"** You just might be seen as a difficult person to someone. Treat the person you consider difficult as if that person is you.

- **Consider the fact that this person might be someone you were designed to help.** There might be something about your personality that can help make them a better person.

- **Be patient with them and do your best to keep peace.** Be loving and kind and try to understand that something might be happening in their life. Maybe they have been hurt in the past and their behavior is a way to hide the pain. That doesn't excuse their behavior; however, it does shed light on possible reasons why they act the way they do. They might be crying out for help.

- **When you are around them, assume the interaction will be good and approach them with a loving heart.** Greet them with a posture of gentleness and love. Speak softly and kindly to set the tone for the interaction.

Loving and peaceful relationships take work, but it can be done.

Although relationships—personal and work—are complicated, it's possible to live peaceably with difficult people when you try. There are various types of people in the world. The world would be a boring place to live in if everyone were the same.

Communication is a major factor when you're trying to maintain peaceful relationships. A lot of problems can be solved when you sit and have an honest and civil conversation with someone. This isn't always easy to do, especially at work.

Instead of sharing the issue you have with someone else, talk to the person you have the issue with. Be honest about how you feel. Most people want to know when something bothers you.

Be a good listener when someone is sharing an issue they have with you. Try to understand their perspective. Talk about how you can work together to make things better and identify any common ground.

Let go of grudges and be open-minded when you talk to people at work. Assume the best about their intentions until they show you something different.

Putting yourself in the other person's shoes almost always helps you understand difficult situations. Maybe your co-worker is overambitious and says or does things to look good and ends up hurting you in the process.

Maybe your manager is having a hard time at home with a sick family member and is taking it out on employees. Maybe your co-worker is having marital problems or problems with their children, and their behavior is their way of crying out for help.

It takes work to have peaceful relationships, but you can do it with patience, love, and by putting yourself in other people's shoes.

This is only a test.

I once had a manager who had a very emotional style of communication. She would raise her voice, use unkind words, and sometimes even cry. The work environment was so bad that I made the decision to look for another job. I prayed about my decision to leave and also prayed for my manager. Guess what happened in this situation? The Holy Spirit opened my eyes to see that I was the one who needed to change. When my perspective changed, the whole situation changed.

You might not have an emotional manager, but are you in a difficult situation at work right now? Maybe this is a test for you. Maybe your skills, strengths, and abilities are being strengthened through this trial. Maybe there is something you are supposed to learn in this test that will graduate you to a better job later.

Close your eyes and ask yourself the following questions about the "test":

- How can I change my perspective about this difficult situation?

- What lessons should I be learning in this situation that will help me in the future?

- What skill or competency am I gaining in this situation that I will need to be successful in a future role?

Take a look at yourself and do what you need to do to pass the test. There's a great reward for you in the future if you learn the lesson or gain the skill you are gaining in your present position. The test you are experiencing now is building "muscles" you will need to use on better jobs later.

Your current trial period is part of a bigger plan that God has for you.

Personal Reflection

How can I promote peace in my work relationships that are difficult?

Prayer for When You are Dealing with Difficult People

Heavenly Father, please help me make it through the day on this job. I am troubled on every side.
I pray for my manager, my co-workers, and colleagues
that You will help us work together in unity.
God, give me the strength I need to work as if I am working for You.
Lord, if there is something in me that needs to change,
please help me to figure it out and do better.
If there is a lesson I am supposed to learn here or a skill I need to gain,
help me to pass the test.
Thank You for preparing me for the great plans You have for me. Amen.

Bible Verse for When You are Dealing with Difficult People

Do all that you can to live in peace with everyone.
Romans 12:18

CHAPTER 21

When You Are Concerned About Aging

You are seen and you are important.

I stood in line and watched as the store clerk ignored the lady in line to wait on other customers first. It was as if she didn't see the lady standing there. One by one she kept waiting on other customers until the patient lady finally spoke up. "I'm sorry, ma'am, I didn't know you were ready to check out." She then proceeded to check the lady out with her purchase.

I couldn't help but wonder if the incident occurred because the lady appeared to be older, with a head full of gray hair, a cane, and a checkbook she held in her hand.

It's sad, but there are times when older people are treated as if they're invisible. Maybe you have felt that way in a public place where someone pushed you aside and ignored you to take care of a customer who moved quicker.

You're like a hidden gem. You might not be popular or well known, but you have unique qualities that would inspire others. You have treasures inside that cannot be quantified at any price.

You carry a lot of wisdom because of your years of experience. You have life lessons that can be helpful to other people, especially younger people. Whether you are seen by others or not, God sees you and He knows you. He knows you still have something to offer this world.

He knows your time has not come to leave this world because there is more work for you to do. Be prayerful and keep your eyes and ears open for opportunities to share your wisdom with the world. You never know when you might meet someone who needs the knowledge you have from lessons you have learned in life. You could become an unofficial mentor to someone at any given moment.

God created you and He knows all about you. He knows the beginning and end of your story. Enjoy where you are right now and stay in touch with God for guidance. He is still guiding you day by day.

Keep doing what you were born to do.

Maybe you are at an age where you are fearful of what your future holds. Don't worry, your future is bright. There's still a reason to live life to the fullest. Don't let your age stop you.

The reality is that anyone could leave this earth at any age. Nobody knows when their expiration date is. The good news is that you're still here and as long as you are, you still have purpose. There's more for you to accomplish.

Don't get bogged down thinking about your age or the fact that you might not move as quickly as you used to. That's okay, you can still move.

There's still time to pursue your goals—go to school, write a book, learn how to paint, start guitar lessons. You still have gifts and talents inside you to share with others.

Take life one day at a time and live life to the fullest. Pull out the fine China and silverware you have been saving for a special occasion. Wear the expensive jewelry and shoes and go to dinner at a nice restaurant. Spray on the nice perfume after your shower. Do whatever it is you have been wanting to do.

Life perspectives change with time. Things that once bothered you don't bother you anymore. People's opinion of you no longer matters.

What have you always wanted to do but held back due to fear of judgment? Now that you care less about what people think, go ahead and do the thing you've always wanted to do. Let go and be free to be who you want to be and do what you want to do.

If you're already living your purpose and using your gifts and talents, keep doing that. There are still people who need what you have to offer. Your existence will inspire someone to be their authentic self. When they see you living your purpose with no inhibitions, they will want to do the same.

Keep moving, keep hoping, and keep believing, no matter what your age is.

Coloring your gray hair, or not, is your choice.

I looked in the mirror and saw a long white string in my hair. I thought it was a piece of thread and tried to pull it out but then realized it was a strand of gray hair in my head. My reaction surprised me that day—I was grateful to see it. The gray hair told me that I am still here. I made it this far.

Some days, I don't feel that way, though. Sometimes I want to color my gray hair so that it doesn't stand out. On some days, I wish for my hair to blend together in the youthful dark brown it used to be.

Whether you choose to color your gray hair or not is your choice. What's most important is that you feel comfortable in your own skin.

Your gray hair doesn't validate your competence to function in this world. How you feel about yourself is what matters. When you have confidence internally, it will show on your face, in your walk, and how you present yourself.

You are beautiful with or without gray hair because God created you and you have purpose. Be content with who God created you to be. Accept your unique qualities and embrace everything about yourself.

On the days when you love your gray hair, be at peace with letting it show. Don't be bothered by the disapproving looks you might get from people staring at it. There will be those who love your gray and those who do not approve of showing it. It doesn't matter who likes it as long as you do.

On the days when you don't love your gray, be at peace with coloring it. It's your hair and your choice to do what you want with it.

Whether you have gray hair or not, you can be at peace with your identity and love the way you look. You don't need someone else to validate you. Validate yourself.

Do what makes you feel good about yourself and what helps you to walk in confidence—with or without your gray hair showing.

Aging signs are visual representations of God's faithfulness and long life.

When you think about it, aging signs are reflections of God's faithfulness in your life because He allowed you to live long enough to get them.

Wrinkles usually come with aged skin, and you're blessed to age. Your life was not cut short. You are still here. What a testimony of God's goodness for you to still be breathing on your own. Wrinkles represent a life lived full of experiences like laughter, joy, and some pain, marking the passing of time. It means you have some good memories and also painful ones etched into your skin.

Wrinkles are a symbol of a rich life and wisdom you have gained over time. Lines around the eyes and mouth could be viewed as laugh lines or visible reminders of the happy moments in your life.

Nothing shows more self-confidence than fully embracing the natural beauty of aging signs.

Thank God that He has blessed you to live long enough to see wrinkles in your face, sagging body parts, and gray hair. Living long means you're able to have more meaningful relationships with family and friends. Aging signs are visual signs that you're still able to make a positive impact on the world in one way or another.

What groups of people do you have a burden to help? Are there any organizations in your community or online where you can volunteer with these groups? Reach out to see how you can make an impact. Any amount of time you can commit could make a huge difference in someone's life. You are still on a journey of continuous learning and self-improvement. You can still explore new interests and hobbies. Is there something you have always wanted to learn?

You have more time to create wonderful memories. Don't be distracted by the wrinkles, gray hair, and physical limitations. Enjoy life and do what you can do to make a difference.

It's a privilege and an honor to see life from the other end of the spectrum.

The bright side of aging is the ability to view life through a wiser lens. Having experienced many of the situations younger people go through, you're able to see things from a more mature perspective. Seeing life from the wiser end of the spectrum helps you to look at things with more confidence.

Growing older gives you the freedom to be who you want to be without caring about what other people think, if you ever did. You don't waste time wondering or worrying about the opinions of others. You now realize that people will always have an opinion regardless of what you do.

When you're on the other side of life's spectrum, you can look back over your life and see how far you have come, and it makes you grateful for the years you have left.

Now that you're older, you're in an advantage position, able to make decisions with the benefit of hindsight. You have learned from your lessons and can now make better choices and guide others in making good choices as well.

What a blessing it is to be at this point in your life when you can rest in the fact that you have made it! This is an exciting time. It means you can move through the rest of your life in complete boldness and contentment. God has been with you all this time, and He is still with you—loving you, taking care of you. You have come too far for Him to leave you now. He is still right there with you.

Whatever you do, don't stop being who you were created to be. There are people who still need your gifts and talents. There are people who will encounter you—whether in the grocery store, in the walkway, online, in a class, or wherever you are—who will be touched by your unique personality.

Continue to be the person God created you to be.

Your dreams should not stop when you get a certain age.

Age really is just a number. I have seen many 80-year-olds who still walk with a spring in their step. You would never know their age by the energy they exude. I have met aged people who still exercise at a gym every day.

Age shouldn't dictate the choices you want to make when you have a desire to do something. If you're still alive and breathing, you can accomplish whatever you want to do.

The only alternative to getting older is dying. There were probably times throughout your life when you wondered if you would ever grow old. I remember thinking how old fifty sounded when I was a teenager. Now that I am older, fifty sounds young.

Maybe there have been times in your life when you didn't think you would make it out alive. You probably have friends who are no longer here and didn't make it to your age.

The fact that you're still here means you still have time to reach your goals.

You can choose to do something meaningful with the rest of your life like volunteering in your community. You can choose to travel and see the world. Maybe you can do something you have always wanted to do—take a cruise, learn a foreign language, write a book.

Enjoy the rest of your journey, whatever that looks like for you. Keep dreaming and pursuing your goals.

Forget about your age and any limitations you have put on yourself. You can do whatever you make up your mind to do.

Don't let anyone tell you that you're too old to do something you want to do. Your age is irrelevant to whatever you want to accomplish.

Whatever age you are is the perfect age to try something new.

Don't be so concerned about dying that you forget to live.

I have stood at the bedside of relatives and friends who drew their final breaths. I watched the distant gaze of a dying friend as she whispered about visions—people only she could see—moments before she was gone.

When you sit and think about it...death is terrifying. Not because of pain or loss alone, but because of its mystery. What we can be sure of though is that as long as we are still living and breathing, we can still enjoy life.

One way to enjoy life is by celebrating every chance you get. Here are some ways to celebrate:

- **Celebrate the years you've lived on your birthday.** Celebrate the friends you've made and the enemies that made you stronger through the years.

- **Enjoy your journey.** You're still on a journey through life. Enjoy the scenery along the way.

- **Spend time with family and friends.** It doesn't have to be a special occasion, pick a date and host a potluck, game night, or theme party.

- **Revisit meaningful memories.** Look through old greeting cards, photos, reading old love letters, or whatever cherished artifacts you have.

- **Try something new**—gardening, putting a puzzle together, painting, or going to the theatre.

Celebrating life allows you to express your gratitude to God for the blessing of long life. There are so many ways you could celebrate. The key is to do something you enjoy.

Celebrate the good times in your life—old and new.

You are like fine wine.

Wine is made by fermenting grapes, which involves crushing, pressing, and aging the grapes. The fermentation process turns grape juice into wine by converting sugars into alcohol and carbon dioxide.

There are many steps in producing wine—harvesting, crushing, fermentation, clarification, aging, and then bottling. During the aging process, the wine is aged in barrels or tanks to develop its flavor and aroma. Aging is one of the factors that affects wine quality because it impacts the flavor and aroma of the wine.

As you age, you live through many experiences—good and bad—just like the process of making fine wine.

There are times in life when you harvest accomplishments and blessings. There are also times of hardship when you go through trials and lose friends. All of these experiences make you the person you are today.

After the many years of pressing and aging, you are now like fine wine with a sweet aroma and flavor of life. Your life experiences have formed you into the beautiful and wise person you are today.

I don't know about you, but I love the taste and aroma of a glass of fine wine. A nice glass of wine gives an element of elegance and sophistication to the moment. Savor the moment where you are right now. Enjoy the sweet essence of a mature and settled life.

Share the wisdom and knowledge you have gained through the years with others. Do not hide your wisdom in a bushel. Be willing to help others when they seek your guidance.

Let your light shine, don't suppress it. Do what you can to share your light with those around you. You have a lot to share. God can still do new things in your life and through your life.

Personal Reflection

What am I most thankful for at this stage in my life?

What are some things I can do now that I never had a chance to do?

Prayer for When You are Concerned About Aging

Heavenly Father, I thank You that I am still Your child, and
You are still taking good care of me.
Thank You for blessing me to see so many years of life. You have kept me and
protected me, and I am grateful.
Since I am still here, I know You still have work for me to do. I pray that You will
continue to lead me and guide me.
I pray for open doors that should be opened in my life and
closed doors that should be closed.
I pray for divine appointments with people
who will be a blessing to me and I to them.
I pray for health, wealth, and peace.
Thank You for seeing me, loving me, and being with me for the rest of my life.
Amen.

Bible Verse for When You are Concerned About Aging

The glory of the young is their strength;
the gray hair of experience is the splendor of the old.
Proverbs 20:29

Chapter 22

Conclusion

God's love for you is the bright side. When we focus on God's love for us, the light of His love will shine and immediately replace any and every darkness we will ever experience.

Looking on the bright side doesn't mean you walk around wearing rose-colored glasses in a fairytale world. It doesn't mean you ignore the problems or difficult relationships in your life.

Rather, it means you see the problem, but you choose to focus on the positive in every situation, knowing that God is always with you.

Times will get hard. There will be dark days. But when you look on the bright side, you can push through anything and move forward to fulfill your purpose in life.

Ignoring problems won't make them go away. You'll eventually have to address them, or they'll address you through stress on your body and mind

Regardless of what is going on around you and how tough life gets, God is always there. He is always available to love, comfort, guide, and hold your hand through any situation.

God loves you more than you could ever imagine. His love is a personal gift for you. Allow His love to comfort you and help you look on the bright side.

Manage problems through prayer and hope, so that they don't overcome you and keep you in a dark place.

Looking at the bright side means you're able to recognize a hard situation, pray about it, and find good things to focus on until the situation is resolved. This allows you to move forward in hope.

I love how the Bible puts it: *"Casting down imaginations, and every high thing that exalts itself against the knowledge of God and bringing into captivity every thought to the obedience of Christ."*

Jesus is the true light that will push away the darkness. He will help you look on the bright side of every situation, so that you can move forward to fulfill God's purpose for your life.

And now, dear brothers and sisters, one final thing.
Fix your thoughts on what is true, and honorable, and right,
and pure, and lovely, and admirable.
Think about things that are excellent and worthy of praise.
Philippians 4:8

About the Author

April Crimbley is a dynamic and inspiring author with a Bachelor of Science in Business Administration. As a retired training professional, she has developed curricula for major corporations, bringing a wealth of knowledge and experience to her writing. April is also a certified Life and Career Coach, dedicated to helping others live authentically and purposefully by exploring their God-given gifts and talents.

April's passion for affirming individuality and fulfilling one's destiny shines through in her volunteer work as a mentor to young women and a facilitator, conducting interactive and enlightening workshops.

When April is not writing or facilitating workshops, she loves spending time with family, volunteering in the community, and reading other books for lifelong learning and growth.

Learn more about the author at www.AprilCrimbley.com.

Also by April Crimbley

Other Books by April Crimbley

Single Dose: Finding Peace, Fulfillment, and Contentment Being Single
Listed as author, April Harding
ISBN: 978-1-7334011-9-7

From Me to Us: 4 Steps from Single to Married Life
ISBN: 978-1-7334011-0-4 (pbk)
ISBN: 978-1-7334011-1-1 (ebk)
ASIN: B08FBL389T (audiobook)

www.ingramcontent.com/pod-product-compliance
Lightning Source LLC
Chambersburg PA
CBHW030549080526
44585CB00012B/311